UNLOCK THE POWER

SINGAPORE DISCOVERIES

*How Singapore Activates Strengths to Become
the World's Best Place to Do Business*

ISBN-13: 978-1507771624
ISBN-10: 1507771622

VIYA CHEN

Speaker, Author and Strengths Business Coach

The founder of VIABIZ Coaching and Consultancy based in Singapore, Viya is the first Gallup Certified Strengths Coach of Taiwan, an ACC Business Coach, a Senior Consultant, and a Business Leader on ways to improve individual, team, and organizational performance. She has more than 20 years of executive experience at Fortune 100 companies in the management, marketing, sales, research, and non-profit sectors. She has a proven track record in delivering effective multinational strategies to drive brand leadership and sustainable growth across the APMEA region.

Viya has led the Strengths 4 Success program on corporate speaking, facilitating training, and coaching for business leaders and entrepreneurs. She uses a Strengths-Based development philosophy, offering the program in Chinese and English. She regularly speaks to leadership audiences and business leaders in Asia about the importance of activating their strengths and aligning their brand vision to create a culture and brand fueled by purpose. She is a leader in brand strategy and has been quoted as an industry expert in many media and business publications. She helps clients transform their organizations to meet their most critical business needs by implementing best practices in customer and employee engagement, business strategy, strengths-based development, and brand and leadership development.

Viya most recently served as the ExCo Committee of ICF Singapore to develop the Coaching for Community initiative. She helps coaches to support leaders by activating their strengths, clarifying their purpose, and increasing their performance. She holds a Master's Degree in Marketing Communication from Michigan State University in the USA and a Global Leadership Program Certificate from Thunderbird University. She is a Gallup-certified Strengths coach, ACC, ACTP, ACTA. Her personal mission is to be a catalyst for inspiring leaders to transform their organizations and build a platform to support coaches to see and fulfill their dream of impacting the world.

www.StrengthsBusiness.com

CONTENTS

THE SUCCESSFUL PATH OF ACHIEVING GOALS

Vision, such an illusionary and hopeful word.

But nowadays, no matter you are a founder of an enterprise, a proprietor of a brand, or even a leader of a nation, you have to keep this word in mind. Because by describing your visions, you're actually showing people who you are and leading your team to the wonderful realm in your heart. Otherwise, they would have every reason to doubt you and prevent you from getting involved with their lives. As Viya said in the beginning, "to accomplish the future, one must recognize his strengths and depict his visions clearly."

As a leader of an enterprise and a professional adviser in managing brands for clients, I am deeply touched by Viya's missionary spirit. Years of managing experiences and energy from her devoted career as a business coach, along with her insights and storytelling skills, enable her to show us the importance of vision. Furthermore, she is professional and passionate to assist people in finding their own visions.

To my surprise, Viya reached a new level upon enterprise and brand management.

Singapore's policy development, education system, urban planning, financial investment, natural landscape… they all together make a great example that as long as you recognize your strengths and make clear and innovative visions, you can built a small red dot country as prosperous as possible.

I am reviewing Viya's "Success for Strengths" Coaching philosophy over and over again, and the questions she raised: What are my inherited talent? What are my strengths? Do I have any unrealized ambitions? Am I expecting any changes? Or longing for the prospects of the next 10 years? Am I resolved to embrace the future and get started? Am I ready to lead myself or a team, use the power of strengths and plan to fulfill my visions in business and life?

Yes, Yes, Yes. If this is also your answer, let us get together and enjoy a superb experience of achieving goals!

—Margaret Huang, CEO of Leo Burnett Group

EXPLORE THE VALUE OF LIFE

As my friend, Viya has an extraordinary career which is a pride of ethnic Chinese and can not to be replicated. In my entrepreneurial process, many of her viewpoints enlightened my directions and objectives.

It's such an honor to write preface for Viya's new book "*Unlock the Power*". The book discussed the successful development experience of Singapore and the life value within. It refreshed my perspectives on all the efforts I've been made and perseverance I've been given on the things I do best. Meanwhile, I envisioned the next stages of my career and life. We can conclude that excellent leaders who get good use of the superior resource, know their strengths and have visionary plannings will dominate the nation's development. The Singapore government takes its multi-cultural advantage to recruit great talents, manages the people with high moral standards, makes this tiny, red-dot country glow only because they focus on their strengths.

—Eagle Guo,
Chairman of Khouse Real Estate, Taiwan

ACHIEVE SUCCESS THROUGH STRENGTHS LEADERSHIP

As a professional coach with international certification, Viya doesn't know she was already my mentor and coach back to 20 years ago when we were working together in the same corporate group. At the time, she was a predecessor to me and solved many puzzles for me. She stepped from Taiwan to the globe, has the experience of taking care of an enterprise which covers a quarter of the globe. She has been so resolved to be a Strengths-driven Coach that it reflects in every aspects of her work, family life and career. Singapore started with great vision, the governments made feasible strategies and fulfilled commitments, all the people act practically. Through Viya's life and business experience in APMEA region, we could see the great achievements they have made that dwarfed the world. The best sections of this book are those chapters with Viya's coaching philosophy and strategic thinking involved. There are powerful questions in her "Unlock the Power: 90-Day Challenge Workbook". Those good questions were properly raised for readers to inspect their own visions according to the development of

Singapore. I enjoy the process when I can read and learn on one hand, know my strengths and inspect my visions and make sure they are gradually realizing on the other hand. Those who want to be professional managers or leaders can find numerous good cases of maximizing your inherited talents or limited resources in this book. We don't have to be perfect at everything, but we can always learn lessons from history, learn how Singapore convert their finite resources into strengths with high efficiency.

Abby Shieh, General Manager of Ogilvy &
Mather Public Relations Company

STRENGTHS

ACTIVATE THE STRENGTHS FOR SUCCESS

Do you want to be successful in your life?
What do you know about leveraging your strengths?
What can you do to fulfill your vision of your life?

Most of us dream of achieving success or fulfilling the purpose of our business or life. I have learned many great lessons from *The Little Red Dot*— Singapore. Perhaps the greatest lessons are also the four major focuses you need when unlocking the power of your business and your life:

- Exploring strengths

- Envisioning a clear future

- Engaging resources

- Empowering strategic actions

In Singapore, one of the most internationalized countries in the world, I heard my inner voice calling for change. This guided me to achieve my second career in life— becoming a Strengths-based Business Coach. If you are interested in exploring the power of changing nations and learning how coaching questions will help you get closer to your goals without limitations, please join me in the journey of 'Unlocking the Power".

In 2007, a fortuitous opportunity made my entire family (my husband who had been a media worker for 20 years and my two sons who were respectively in middle school and primary school) immigrate from Taiwan to Singapore, known as *Lion City*.

This occurred because McDonald's headquarters appointed me to manage the brand and marketing activities in the Asia-Pacific, the Middle East, and Africa region. After that, I went from promoting hamburgers and cokes, popularizing Hello Kitty and Coke glasses, and spreading joy and laughter in Taiwan to doing these things and making billions dollars decision in more than 20 countries. This great opportunity expanded my transcultural visions to become an international, professional marketer and businesswoman.

Singapore, a city known as *The City in a Garden* and *A Shopping Paradise* that includes multi-ethnic cultures, is my second home. I learned its 50-year history, including how it transformed from a poor village into one of the leading financial hubs in the world. The Economist Intelligence Unit (EIU) ranked Singapore as number one out of 82 countries for its "efficient and open economy". The tiny Asian island nation has been at the top of the rankings for seven consecutive years, since year 2008. Singapore also topped the World Bank's ease of doing business report, which looked at 189 countries.

What's underneath the success is a courageous spirit with perseverance and tolerance. This unique cultural feature brought this miraculous country to life. Its developing history contains the dreams of many generations. The aesthetics of this city are gorgeous, and its stories worth reading.

In 2015, Singapore is celebrating the 50th anniversary of its independence. I invite you to celebrate with us by learning how you can achieve success through the story of this nation, which has surpassed its size, triumphed despite historical adversity, and overcome numerous other obstacles.

CHANGE IS ALWAYS A CHOICE

Singapore is an island country, but its position as a business hub supported me in expanding my work to cover a quarter of the globe. Departing from this little red dot, I took business trips around the world and felt the charm of every city. Then I deeply realized that the size of the future you belong to originates in your mindset.

Your greatest realized dreams are based on how specific your visions are, how you define your purpose in life, and what your expectations of your wealth or career are. They aren't based on the size of the country you're from. Life varies from person to person since every individual has different talents and visions, which create the uniqueness of every life.

My first career satisfied my longing for travelling with continuous business trips. I preferred wandering through the streets of every new city. One year, I spent 200 days travelling from one city to another and experiencing life around the world, and I never got tired.

Singapore gave me excitement and desires. After getting an overall idea of the policy of the environment by learning it in person, I started to understand how it made full use of its inherited but limited resources to build this *City in a Garden*, a favorable place for international professionals to live, work, and invest.

When my family first moved to Singapore, we saw Sentosa, the world's most beautiful and desirable residential area. Not only have we been amazed by the spectacular scenery and landscaping, we've also been astounded by the master plan of its organization and design. The Singapore government spent 20 years planning it and started from scratch, determined to implement their land reclamation project. They ultimately built a distinctive, open, safe, luxury villa area. It's evidence that you can build the world's most desirable real estate from nothing. We were envisioning that we would stay on this island from the first time we visited it. The third year I worked in Singapore, we moved from the Bukit Timah area to Sentosa. Our dream came true.

Our newly built condo has a view of the sea from the balcony, where one can watch large freighters full of cargo come and go through the port as if they are soldiers showing off their power. Ferryboats sailing from Harbourfront to Indonesia, private houseboats, yachts, and fishing boats all crowd in and out. The back balcony faces the yacht club, and private boats with all kinds of sizes dock at the barge berth. On idle days, I send the kids to school, walk along the coast through the dock toward the rising sun, enjoy the breeze blowing to my face, see the white boats and blue sky that enhance each other's beauty, and embrace every joyful day.

The residents are coming from everywhere in the world. Some of them have been sent here with their families by international businesses; others may have settled in just because they enjoy the place. They chat with each other when they encounter by chance, telling different stories and discovering different lifestyles. This way of communicating reminds me how many diverse alternatives there are in life.

Someone wise once said, "In a lifetime, one decision triggers another, one coincidence leads to another. Thus, there is no accident, one way is always followed by another, you can never go back." Then why not recognize ourselves, change our pace, turn to a different channel, see different colors, hear different voices? Life is a journey of experience unto itself.

A GOAL IS A DREAM WITH A DEADLINE

People have been on the move since time immemorial, but it's human nature to stay in their comfort zone. At the beginning, change requires adjustment, and it is always accompanied by confusion and setbacks. However, only change can help create new connections, possibilities and visions for life.

It was not easy to leave a multi-national corporation, which is definitely a comfort zone for most white collar people. However, it was Singapore that affected this change. This country made me realize that I could do it, just as this small country with scarce resources turned into a country that never ceases to amaze the world. As long as we are able to create a vision and awar our strengths, all of us can create miracles. Our lives are built from all those images we once had about the life we dreamt of.

Visions of Singapore gave me strength to believe I could change. As long as one has a dream, moves towards clear goals, does not lose curiosity and interest in new things and has the will and determination to prevail, one will always encounter an opportunity to discover their purpose and create a new life.

Things that we are interested in always provide us with the motivation to learn, to keep moving forward and explore ever deeper. When we are young, we always listen to the sound of our dreams, but as we grow, we slowly forget how to pursue these dreams.

A goal is a dream with a deadline. How can we realize this dream in our hearts? How should we listen to the sound of enthusiasm? What's the best way to focus, persist and stay true to our wish to achieve the goal in our life?

During one coaching session, the coach asked me to make sentences using "I am..., I want..., I will..." Without thinking, I answered: "I am a visionary and futurist! I want to stand on the platform that faces the world. I will walk at my own pace, live up to work and life values, and create a platform to help others see and achieve their dreams."

Thus, I started my second career. I left a safe and secure job at a big company and started my own coaching and consultancy business. I obtained my international professional certification and focused on developing leadership and vision to become a masterful strengths coach. I gave speeches, coached, and wrote books. The former recipient, who carried out other's plans, truly became an architect who builds dreams. When I wrote out my vision to collect and weave dreams, Singapore, this small red dot, became clear in front of my eyes.

The goal is a specific, measurable and timely dream with a deadline. The steps to focus on one's vision and live up to one's dreams – whether it is a country looking to bring good to its people, a company looking to bring benefits to its customers, or an individual looking to bring change to their life – are all the same.

I've heard it said, "As long as you see clearly, influence others with your enthusiasm, know your strengths, face obstacles, follow prescribed orders, spare no effort, you will achieve your dreams." As Leo Burnett, the founder of a well-known advertising company put it, "When you reach for the stars, you may not quite get one, but you won't come up with a handful of mud either." Another entrepreneur put it a different way, "If you cannot give up on what you like, you should try and make others see that you exist."

If you want to try new ideas, don't hold back. In my experience as a professional coach, I've seen that if you want to break through your old life routine and get new ideas, you should take a break, reflect on the trails you have followed, listen to your heart, be aware of the conflicts, discover your thoughts, and consider the sentiments inside you. Only then can you find a different meaning of life.

At different stages of life, make a plan and don't forget to ask yourself, "What is the meaning of my life? What experiences do I want to have? What are the steps for living up to my dream?" If you have a dream, you will naturally feel a corresponding passion. Stare at your vision, but don't just stare at it, and don't give up on yourself.

It's like the miracle of Singapore, without abundant resources or a beautiful natural landscape. People in this country showed the world the power of dreams with clear vision and persistent action. Trips to the unknown are not always perfect; not everything is smooth. However, if you walk toward your vision and follow your dreams, you will not regret the life you have.

BELIEVE IN A BETTER YOU

The job of a coach is to find strengths in clients and enrich their lives by interacting with them. It is a comprehensive process to help them see their future clearly. This is true whether a coach's client is a country, a society, a company, a family, or an individual. In order to fulfill an ideal future, you need to learn about yourself, explore your inherited talents, develop your vision, and start from a conceptual plan.

It is natural for us to fear what we do not know. You must first have the desire to succeed above anything else. Then you will have the chance to become a better you. Passion enables you to make a good assessment of your strengths and weaknesses. The most effective leaders are always investing in strengths, surrounding themselves with the right people, and maximizing their team. Leaders also know how to help others harness their strengths for greater personal success. When you become clearer on where you want to go and what life you want to live, you will set up cyclical plans, act and analyze in the prescribed way, and understand your followers' needs. Then you will achieve your dreams gradually.

The coaching mode developed from Exploring Strengths will give you unique insights to help people understand, apply, and integrate the results of these strengths into their lives and careers. This process will guide the potential value inside one's head. Through emotional projection from one's heart, one can develop the blueprint of one's vision. At this point, the gut needs to be driven by passion and guide the action of one's hands. Then, with guidance and motivation from a Strengths Coach, the individual or enterprise will explore possibilities and finally take strategic action!

Through a coaching process, one should find Five Abilities to drive change in individuals or enterprises to achieve their goal. These are all findings that need to be discovered while coaching clients. Your vision will guide you to move forward if it is a clear one. The story of the success of Singapore and Malaysia will show you the five abilities that you must develop:

- IQ (Intelligence Quotient) to solve problems

- EQ (Emotional Quotient) to face problems

- PQ (Patience Quotient) to see problems

- CQ (Creation Quotient) to change problems

- SQ (Social Quotient) to surpass problems

These abilities are all connected with each other. This tells us that no matter what kind of future a country, a society, a family, or an individual wants, developing a vision is imperative.

OPENING INNER DIALOGUES

The shape of one's life is based on one's imagination. As long as we have visions for life, move toward goals with a clear mind, stay interested and curious to the future, and persist with a practical attitude, we can find our own dreams and create greater opportunities to realize them.

A change of vision can directly affect the state and pace of one's life. As amazing visionaries, Singapore has not only changed themselves but have had a great impact on the entire planet. By discovering and learning strengths-driven methods, one can build a system that includes the purposes, visions, and risks of managing one's life or business. By changing and executing these methods, individuals can increase their chance to realize their dreams.

As a professional coach, I hope readers can find the motivation to change through my coaching questions and guidance attached my the workbook of "90-Day Challenge". Furthermore, they should be able to see the value of investing and developing their talents, use strengths to transform their relationships, and overcome obstacles, weaknesses, and vulnerabilities. They can also establish a clear direction to make the changes that will get them closer to their vision.

CHAPTER 1:

TRANSFORMATION

SEE THE POWER OF VISION

"The power of imagination makes us infinite."

—John Muir

Do what you feel passionate about, enjoy an amazing lifestyle, take your life or business to the next level. Become empowered. Be the best version of yourself.

Vision, also called the imagery of inspiration, is the process of creating an image of our desired future. It will be the starting point of transformation. From this point, you will identify the needed change, create an ongoing vision to guide the change through inspiration, and execute the change with commitment. You cannot control the future, but you can plan for it. Create a clearly defined picture of what you really want in life. This picture should be so vivid that you could actually draw it. Visualize the ending you want at the beginning of the process. This helps us to navigate our way through the journey.

Vision is an intuitive picture that matches our passion. Creativity is often defined as the ability to bring possibilities into existence that are new, different, or inspired. When you see this picture in your imagination, it should energize you right away. Visualization allows the client to imagine themselves without fears, barriers, or restraints. Because of its tangibility, it makes us feel empowered to shape the direction of our future.

Turning effective strengths into action starts by thinking big but starting small. Look for reproducible strategies. When people realize a dream or a desire, they prove that they were able to visualize their most attainable goal and implement it. As you've probably heard it said, "Even if you hit a home run once, you won't win the game unless you can do it again and again and again".

Neuroscience shows that instinct performs a leading role when making most decisions. This research has proven that imaginative play is one of the most direct means of activating our creativity and problem-solving abilities.

A gut feeling is a sensation that instantly appears in our subconscious without us being fully aware of the underlying reasons for this occurrence. This can shape our tendency to either pursue goals that are about performance or goals that are about progress. Goals that are about performance are based on the feedback of others, like performance reviews or grades. Goals that are about progress are based on our vision of the future.

The power of positive thinking can create empowerment, while the feeling of intimacy develops a sense of engagement. By contrast, there might be times when things don't work out or are not sufficiently satisfying. Our intuitive feeling might convey demotivation to our brain, which would discourage our heart in the pursuit of our goals. Then our guts would feel powerless and unprogressive.

The processes of experiencing empowerment will initiate a structure for the creation of positive energy to guide decisions about your business and your life. By knowing your strengths, you will be able to motivate and lead yourself effectively.

We all have different 'be-good' performance goals or 'get-better' mastery goals. These goals keep us moving forward. When we pursue performance goals, our energy is directed at achieving a particular outcome, which is often tied closely to our sense of self-worthiness and validation. This makes us look and feel smart, talented, and desirable. Performance goals are characterized by an all-or-nothing quality; you either reach the goal or you don't. And then we judge ourselves according to whether or not we are successful. On the other hand, the desire to get better – to develop or enhance our skills and abilities – is a mastery goal. We judge ourselves in terms of the progress we are making. Am I improving? Am I learning? Am I moving forward at a good pace? It's less about a one-time performance, and more about one's performance over time.

The definition of 'demotivation' is the feeling people get when they lose their enthusiasm or interest, often due to an outside force. Frequently, when people focus hard on a problem, they become stressed about it. A demotivated thinker normally has the perspective that they do not have the necessary freedom from constraints, the ability to move projects forward, or the ability to manage their own time. They don't feel recognized by their colleagues and peers and cannot find the opportunity for personal growth.

Occasionally we feel stuck in a situation in our life and can't see a way forward. If you can discern this perspective and reframe it, then you can free yourself up to find new solutions and move on.

START YOUR ENGINES

Corporations strive to give customers the feeling that they'll have a glimpse into a different world if they buy a certain product. A unique brand experience is a factor of brand value. It contains people's sense of identity about the additional meanings of a brand, and it motivates passionate people to support and participate in the brand's promise, appreciate brand value, and pay for the offered products or services. When buying a certain product, customers are buying a different lifestyle or experience within it.

Consider a nation or a city that develops itself without clear plans and a great vision of its future. Without thinking about what it wants the experience of its citizens or visitors to be, it barely stands the chance of being built with distinction and pride.

For the last few years in The Global Competitiveness Yearbook, The World Economic Forum has named Singapore one of the top three most competitive economic entities in the world. If we look into the reasons for this level of success from Singapore in the international world today, we will find the reasons that it has become one of the world's best places to do business and one of the top cities to live, work, and invest in. We will discover the following eight characteristics of its transformation:

1. Strengths-Driven Solutions

Recognize, analyse, and develop strengths. Create blueprints, stay alert to outside threats, and proceed with the single-minded direction of achieving success.

2. Explicitly Shared Vision

   Determine and implement unequivocal visions to make the country more competitive.

3. Maximize Leaders' Influence

   A leader should guide a team with his or her unique personality, passion, determination, and execution.

4. Believe in Intellectual Analysis

   Analyze the problems and advantages with a scientific attitude, and focus on solutions.

5. Develop a Blueprint

   Through visualized communication and guidance, let the followers participate in creating the blueprints of cities.

6. Dare to Dream

   Put dreams into practice with pragmatic execution, and make great differences one step at a time. A goal is a dream with a deadline.

7. Focus on External Threats

   Open your eyes to the whole world, pay attention to external trends and environmental changes, and prevent excessive resource consumption internally.

8. Appreciation and Celebration

   Maintain unique traditions of racial integration, and make celebrations public. The city-state is an organism that wants a dream of success that it can support.

ENVISION THE RIGHT OUTCOMES

When you read this book, your life path may not change. But through the successful experience of Singapore how it turns from a village to the world's best place to do business, you can find the strengths-driven power to transform limited resources into great advantages. In whichever path to the future you utilize this inspiration, you can start the practice of creating your own dream life!

In the following chapters, you will learn how Singapore created the model of success that allowed visions to bring them great achievements.

AMAZING MILESTONES OF SINGAPORE

1. In *The Global Competitiveness Yearbook 2014*, the World Economic Forum named Singapore "the most competitive country in the world" and "the least corrupt economic entity in Asia".

2. In the *Global Business Environment Report* of the World Bank, Singapore was named "the world's most convenient place to do business" in 2014.

3. For the last fourteen consecutive years, the American Business Environment Risk Assessment Corporation has ranked Singapore second on its list of the world's most promising cities for investments.

4. Mercer ranked Singapore second in urban infrastructure in its *2014 Worldwide Quality of Living*.

5. Ranked fourth in the World Financial Centres Index in 2014, Singapore is Asia's leading financial, service, and shipping center.

6. A high level of international trade, large international telephone traffic, and large numbers of international tourists have made Singapore one of the most internationalized countries.

7. With only 710 square kilometers of territorial area, Singapore is one of the 20 smallest countries in the world, but it ranked in the world's third richest country.

8. Singapore has one of the lowest unemployment rates in the world. It was only 2% in 2014.

9. Singapore is one of the world's most successful cities in greening.

10. Singapore boasts the world's third largest foreign exchange trading center.

11. Singapore's density of millionaire households ranked third in the world, behind only Qatar and Switzerland. It has the world's highest super-rich population.

AMAZING MILESTONES OF MALAYSIA

1. Named one of the Top 25 countries in Global Competitiveness, and it continues to rise.

2. Ranked 9th in countries with the largest number of super-growth companies, showing the willingness of medium-sized and large enterprises to set up in Malaysia.

3. Ranked 26th in the Global Network Readiness Index.

4. As the world's largest producer and exporter of oleochemicals, Malaysia has abundant oil and gas resources.

5. The world's second largest producer and exporter of crude palm oil.

6. Ranked as the second most-visited Asian country in 2013.

Countless experiences and examples tell us that strengths-driven goals exist in every human being on some level. Through exploring the power of vision, you will be guided and inspired to find your strengths and realize your dreams.

Through observing and recording as a coach, I saw the strategic approaches in Singapore to realize these visions. The execution of this vision brought them the achievements they have today.

Immigrants have been struggling for their dreams with sweat, blood, and tears throughout several generations. Clarify what matters most, calculate the time and put the goals on the calendar. "Dreams rise up Singapore and Malaysia in Asia, they are stepping forward towards the vision, firmly and vigorously."

DISCOVER YOUR STRENGTHS

People don't usually know a fun fact about Singapore. It only has one railway station. This is probably unique in the world. The station is located in Woodlands, a suburban town in northern Singapore, where you can take the train all the way to Kuala Lumpur. The railway extends north to Bangkok, Thailand, with a total length of 1,800 kilometers.

At present, China is speeding up the construction of its international railway from Yunnan to Laos, which is expected to be completed in 2015. When it's done, a total length of 3,900 km of railway from Singapore to Kunming can be incorporated into the Trans-Asian Railway Network. Singapore and Malaysia have made plans to invest three billion ringgit to build a high-speed rail from Kuala Lumpur to Singapore, which will shorten the ride to just 90 minutes. Between these two plans, you can get a glance at the development trends of the Association of South-East Asian Nations (ASEAN), an international political organization.

Borders will not disappear on the economic map, but the boundaries between countries has gradually blurred. In the globalized 21st century, the development of a country is no longer dependent on hard work behind closed doors. To compete with other economic entities, we must establish regional advantages through cooperation and resources that are complementary with neighboring countries.

For nearly five decades, there has been both competition and cooperation between Singapore and Malaysia. Today, Singapore has become a dazzling cosmopolitan city, while things went differently on the other side of the bridge in Malaysia. During the change from the 20th century to the 21st century, an era of global cooperation and mutual benefit has arrived. A regional strategic cooperation has replaced a sharply divided situation.

For example, ASEAN was established to fight against the expansion of communism during the Cold War. After fifty years of development, the countries that were communist back then have joined, one after another. It has now become a large political and economic organization called ASEAN Ten Plus Three. These three countries (China, Japan, and Korea) will follow the example of the

European Union and be converted into the ASEAN Community in 2015. Under this cooperative and mutually beneficial atmosphere, the Malaysian government's economic construction has become more resilient and pragmatic.

The Comprehensive Development Plan in 2006 was to learn from the development experience of Shenzhen and extend Iskandar into Singapore's Special Economic Zone. It aimed to extend Singapore's living area and create an educational, recreational, low-density industrial center.

Currently, the Special Economic Zone has entered an extensive phase of construction. Hundreds of billions of ringgit have been put in place, which include Singapore National funds and private investment funds.

The future development of Singapore and Iskandar can no longer be treated separately. However, we will see if this dynamic duo, under the ASEAN Community framework, will step onto the world stage with a mutually beneficial urban style.

A LEADER IS A BRAND

One can't speak of Singapore without mentioning two men. Stamford Raffles is known as "the father of Singapore", and Lee Kuan Yew is the founder of the Republic of Singapore. Although they belong to different centuries, their adventurous spirit and indomitable willpower have unshakable historic influence on the development of Singapore.

In the 15th century, the Age of Discovery, European powers started to contest overseas colonies and extend sea power. In the 17th century, the Dutch colonised the island of Java and constantly expanded outwards to the Malay Peninsula and Sumatra Islands. In order to break the Dutch monopoly, England joined in the colonization of Malaysia in the 18th century. Then the war began.

In 1819, in order to find a trade post with more geographical advantages, Raffles established a new colony at the southern tip of the Malay Peninsula – Singapore, which used to belong to the Kingdom of Johor. This move greatly challenged the Dutch hegemony in the area in a way that would probably lead to a war. Meanwhile, the British government disapproved of the declaration of war over a tiny island and ordered Raffles to retreat from Singapore. However, Raffles believed in the unique geographical advantages and development potential of Singapore. He put great effort into convincing the Indian Viceroy to argue with the Dutchmen, pointing out that Singapore did not legally belong to Malacca.

Because of his persistence and hard work, Britain gradually understood the importance of Singapore. In the Anglo-Dutch Treaty of 1824, Singapore was officially assigned to be a British colony. It was after the British colonization that Singapore developed into an important international trading port. Singapore would not be able to have today's prosperity without Raffles' insight and perseverance. He deserves people's respect for initiating such a great beginning of Singapore's prosperity.

Jumping ahead to August 9, 1965, the Malaysian Parliament unanimously passed a resolution to expel Singapore out of the Federation. Singapore's Prime Minister Lee Kuan Yew could not help but shed tears while declaring his country's independence on television. They were not happy tears, but tears of not knowing the future. For a tiny island with nearly no natural resources (including drinking water), it was difficult to imagine surviving among those powerful competitors.

However, eras, no matter how hard they are, produce heroes. Lee Kuan Yew was Prime Minister of Singapore for 30 years until 1990. During that time, he led the people of Singapore to construct the country with great effort. These efforts included the promotion and development of Jurong Industrial Park, the construction of a large number of Housing and Development flats, the foundation of the Corrupt Practices Investigation Bureau, and major economic and educational reform.

This series of policy measures allowed Singapore to gradually be reborn and become one of the most wealthy and prosperous countries in Asia. The Little Red Dot was finally shining on the world stage.

Lee Kuan Yew was born in a Chinese family in Singapore and had a British education. This causes him to use his strengths realistically and reasonably. On the other hand, he upholds Oriental Confucianism with a concerned, responsible mind. He likes to share his vision and upholds practical values. He is always able to distinguish right from wrong. He chooses what is good, holds fast to it, and hates evil as an enemy. These distinctive characteristics molded Singapore's brand and its development features.

CITY IN A GARDEN WITH SOUL

Located in downtown Singapore, Garden by the Bay was officially opened in July 2012. Its architecture was meant to define Singapore as a City in a Garden. The design concepts present an awe-inspiring vision for the future of the city. Walking under the towering trees in the garden reminds you of James Cameron's work in *Avatar*. Marveling at these aesthetic achievements, you can't help but think about how to develop a harmony between technology and nature in the future.

From the moment the garden was completed, a brand new landscape was incorporated into the city's skyline. At a total cost of 810 million Singapore dollars, the garden covers an area equivalent to 177 football fields. More than 80 percent of the world's plant species have been utilized in the garden. There are plants from every continent grown under different climatic conditions, even including some rare or endangered plants. This is the dream garden that a country could give its people, with the vision of huge resources and efforts built around Miracles in Singapore are not only reflected in the figures on economic growth. They are also evident in another impressive achievement in a country with the second highest population density in the world: a greening rate of nearly 50 percent.

"Build a garden-like city." For this vision, Lee Kuan Yew advocated that all citizens plant trees in 1963. At the time, Singapore's economy was in an initial stage with a list of innumerable things that needed to be done. Planting trees didn't seem like it should've been a priority since it would take several years to create shade. However, in order to change the harsh and barren environment into a better living space for future citizens, he led Singaporeans to plant 1.5 million trees on the island. A skyscraper can be built in three to five years, while a forest requires half a century, perseverance, and patience.

Trees are the soul of a city. Today, Singapore is full of luxuriant and towering trees. Insects and birds can be heard even in the busiest spots on Orchard Road. How could this Garden City exist without vision and persistence in those early years?

Singapore is now a highly urbanized modern society. However, when it comes to developing urban construction in harmony with nature, it is easier said than done. It was sheer determination that achieved today's greening miracle in Singapore.

FAST FACTS ABOUT SINGAPORE

Singapore is an island nation, as well as a city-state, in Southeast Asia. It is located 137 kilometers north of the equator on the southern tip of the Malay Peninsula, adjacent to the south of the Malacca Strait. It contains the connecting channel between the Pacific and Indian Oceans. In the south, Singapore Strait neighbours Indonesia, and Johor Strait connects Malaysia with the Johor-Singapore Causeway in the north. In addition, the main island accounts for over 90% of its territory. The terrain slopes gently throughout the nation; the highest point is Bukit Timah Hill at 164 meters above sea level.

The climate is hot and humid throughout the year without significant changes in temperature. The average maximum temperature is about 32 ° C, and the minimum temperature is 25 ° C. The rainy season is from November to January each year. A heavy rainfall often occurs in the afternoon, but it washes the streets quickly and subsides within the time it takes to drink a cup of coffee.

Singapore is a nation of immigrants. According to demographic data, Singapore had only 303,000 population in 1911, 72% of which were Chinese. Although the Chinese dominated the population, the Malays settled in Singapore before them. In the early years after independence, the island had almost no natural resources except granite. There was no self-sufficient surface water, not even groundwater. Before independence, Singapore attracted a large number of other immigrants, mostly from Fujian province, but also from Chaoshan, Guangdong, Hakka, and Hainan. Singapore, China, and Taiwan are currently the only countries that have a majority of people with Chinese ethnicity.

Singapore's national flower is the light purple Vanda Miss Joaquim, which has four beautiful petals that represent the four major ethnic groups and language families. As part of an overall effort to foster national pride and identity, it is popularly known, free flowering, colorful, and attractive. This elegant and refined flower symbolizes the modesty, vitality, diligence, and courage of the Singaporean people.

Nowadays, new immigrants are arriving from everywhere. Data shows that in the past decade, Singapore's population has increased by a quarter. It exceeded 5.5 million as of 2014. In order to avoid an aging society and workforce crisis that could drag down the economy, the Singapore government distributed a population policy white paper in 2013. It explicitly set a 30% growth target of 6.9 million by 2030.

Not only is Singapore a multi-language society, it welcomes free and active religious activities. Different races and religions coexist harmoniously, presenting diversified cultural characteristics. Many different beliefs living together in mutual respect and tolerance is one of the most prominent features of Singapore.

While local Singaporeans feel superior pride about their citizenship, the government hopes to introduce more effective options for future needs. The growth rate of new immigrants is much higher than the local population growth rate. The latter is as low as 1-2%. Therefore, the number of new immigrants may soon exceed the number of current local citizens.

Some native Singaporeans may seek less populated areas in other countries or choose to live in a less competitive, non-urban environment, or choose to live in Malaysia because it has a lower cost of living. They commute to work in the city every day. This kind of personnel flow forms the unique population structure and eclectic nature of Singapore.

UNLOCK THE POWER OF THE RED DOT

Continuous visions and dreams make Singapore an amazing red dot. Here are some developing strengths to create a more vivid picture of the city.

Optimized Blueprints:

- With a total area of only 714 square kilometers, Singapore has created 20% of its territory by reclaiming land from the sea since 1950. It has the world's second highest population density, just below Monaco with an area of 1.95 square kilometres. Although urbanization narrows down the rainforest area, 23% of the land is reserved to protect forests and nature. This is considered significant in terms of urban greening. There are over 300 parks and 4 nature reserves in Singapore. Forests are mainly contained in the Bukit Timah Nature Reserve. Integrated planning has avoided over-crowdedness and achieved great success in urban greening.

- Singapore is also one of Asia's leading financial, service, and shipping centers. Through large banks from various countries working together, Singapore currently has more than 600 local and foreign financial institutions. According to the Dow Jones Index in 2014, Singapore was ranked the world's fourth largest financial center, behind New York, London, and Tokyo. The city's capital market depth and liquidity are its keys to financial success. The SGX (Singapore Exchange) is one of the only capital markets in the Asia-Pacific region that boasts more than 800 listed companies. Singapore is the world's third largest foreign-exchange trading center. Excluding Japan, Singapore has become the largest market of real estate investment trusts (REITs) in Asia. The bond market is also growing remarkably.

- Singapore actively develops tourism, which accounts for a significant proportion of the overall economic structure. Tourists are mainly from Europe, America, Japan, China, and other Southeast Asian countries. The annual tourist population is over 14 million people. An average of nearly 40,000 visitors a day are coming to Singapore for consumption and entertainment.

- Singapore is the third-largest oil refining center in the world. Since 2006, the energy and petrochemical industry has become a pillar of industry in Singapore's economy. Jurong Island is the center of the energy and petrochemical industry. It is one of the world's 10 largest petrochemical bases. Currently, over 100 major global petroleum, petrochemical, and special chemical companies are equipped with factories on the island.

- Singapore is also one of the world's busiest ports. It connects more than 200 shipping routes with over 600 other ports in 123 countries and regions. In 2013, it had the carrying capacity of nearly 32.6 million TEU (twenty-foot equivalent unit). This made it the world's second largest port after Shanghai, which had the capacity of 33.6 million TEU.

- The output value of Singapore's aviation industry is 70 billion Singapore dollars, comprising a quarter of the Asia-Pacific aviation maintenance market. The number of employees is approximately 18,000. The biennial Singapore Air Show is Asia's largest and most influential, as well as the world's third largest.

- In order to be a global aviation hub, Singapore especially planned the development of 'Seletar Aerospace Park', which is expected to be completed in 2018. As a dedicated aviation industrial park, it will cover an area of 320 hectares. This park will provide services for the maintenance, repair, operations, design, and manufacturing of large aircraft systems and components, as well as the entirety of light aircraft. Singaporeans are looking forward to it offering commercial and general airline services and regional aviation education, research, and training.

- Foreign tourists, workers, and investors are attracted to Singapore because of its multiculturalism, its low crime rate, and its national image as a beautiful garden city. The gross domestic product (GDP) per capita ranked third in the world with more than 60,000 USD. This was higher than the United States with 48,387 USD, Japan with 34,740 USD, and Malaysia with 15,568 USD, which respectively ranked 7th, 25th and 59th.

- Under thorough housing management policies, 88% of residents have their own property. Some even have a second residency that can be leased to new immigrants or foreigners. Thus they can collect rents as passive income, which means fewer worries in retirement.

- Singapore's government regulates with high ethical standards. This is reflected in the supervision of people's daily behavior. In order to keep the garden city neat, beautiful, and secure, the government banned chewing gum. When making a free trade agreement with the United States in 2003, the ban on chewing gum was listed as a key issue during bilateral negotiations. As a result of the agreement, the prohibition of chewing gum was approved with the exception of gum needed for medical use.

- Singapore implemented tobacco control with high tax rates, hoping to reduce the likelihood of addiction. Such acts as smoking in non-smoking areas, not crossing the street via specified locations like bridges or tunnels, drinking or eating on the subway, or even not flushing the toilet could result in fines. This is a Law-by-Law country, which means obeying the law step-by-step. Singapore may also have the world's most strict anti-drug laws, maintaining the social order with cruel punishment. "The rules" are taken very seriously in Singapore.

Singapore does not have a magnificent landscape. Singapore has never denied that it is a small country that started as a poor fishing village. But with long-term planning, efficiency and execution, shared experiences, trends and knowledge, the government guided Singapore into a new era of growth and prosperity. You have to admire the determination and perseverance to change.

The government has to be concerned if things they are about to do have already been done. This is because plans can't be made only to repeat successes that have already been achieved. Otherwise, you would miss opportunities for creativity. It may be hard to imagine that government officials have been considering various needs of the people step-by-step, such as births, upbringings, marriages, investments, jobs, health care, and retirement living. They are all planned, executed, and implemented in people's lives. Some say Singapore is boring and unoriginal. Well, every coin has two sides. Clever governments have already solved problems before they even occur to most citizens.

FIND YOUR KEYS TO SUCCESS

Singapore defines itself as a gateway from Asia to Europe and America. This includes keeping pace with the times, protecting invention and innovation, resolving to support entrepreneurs, and continuing to play a major role in the regional economy.

The success of Singapore is based on the development of "maximizing strengths", including the establishment of reliance, the pursuit of innovation, the sharing of visions, the dominant forces, internationalization, knowledge, association, and lifestyle. These brand equities have formed a favorable investment environment, so that more and more international business people rest assured in the funds and operations of Singapore.

- Reliability

Singapore's government is known for integrity, high standards, reliability, high productivity, strict law enforcement, and attention to copyrights. These are strategies to win in the international competition of a knowledge-based economy.

Singapore has been maintaining a competitive advantage of low tax and interest rates. Through the orderly development of petrochemicals, energy supply, and green energy integration, it's gradually developing strengths and economic forces.

In recent years, the development of "the future Singapore" program for urban life, social welfare, population aging, life sciences, and other related products and services are under research and planning.

- Innovation

Most people would not think of Singapore as a creative country, since its art, film, painting, theatre, and fashion are currently not particularly impressive on the world stage. However, creativity comes from cultural strengths, while innovation grows with time. Singapore creates opportunities with education and encourages breakthrough thinking. It cultivates new immigrants and attracts talents with a globalized mind, making the city image one with a green outdoor landscape.

The greening corridor around the island converts problems into opportunities by creating a stunning water supply industry and splendid land reclamation. How can you not admire the innovation of this country? Singapore focuses on creating and adding high-value strengths, turning fantasy into reality by changing the rules of the game with careful and whole-hearted action.

- Sharing visions

Management guru Peter Drucker once said, "One should update his professional knowledge every two years and reestablish his basic capabilities every four years."

The government of Singapore has its own rules to achieve success. It attracts excellent young talents with high salaries and requires integrity, hard work, and great performances from them. Leaders are committed to living in the city, where they make a brand of themselves. The ever-changing city skyline is always attracting attention. The management of a country concerns the well-being of millions of people. It's important to always lead the people a few small steps ahead, so that they can see the government's vision and believe that they can keep up with it.

In the era of "knowledge explosion and experience devaluation", today's intelligence will turn into common knowledge tomorrow. Countries need to refresh their viewpoints and explore new trends. In the borderless world of information, the real-time sharing platform is changing rapidly. For example, the Singapore Government created the vision of being an Intelligent Nation in 2015. By gradually attracting followers, this would have the opportunity to take the lead in the "knowledge economy" of the competitive world.

- Guiding forces

A good government has the ability to point out obstacles blocking the development of its society and come up with strategies accordingly. More importantly, it proves to the people that these policies can bring positive changes, such as constructive communication and social consensus cohesion. Thus, people can trust and support their government, which ensures implementation of important, long-term policies. In international negotiations, this prevents censure from domestic society and strong pressures from foreign parties.

Social consensus does not come from the air. It depends on whether the policy is implemented and if social problems are effectively solved. It needs time to prove if the government has the right guiding forces for policy-making.

- Internationalization

Singapore keeps attracting foreign investors to its plans for wealth and growth by showing them the abundant cultures, sustained growth of the economy, internationalized employment opportunities, and social tolerance. In fact, many international investment companies think of Singapore as a platform for long-term real estate investment and financial development with promising profits and reasonable transactions. With the impact of a growing population and economic globalization, more and more people are investing in the land and real estate business.

- Intellectual factor

Singapore's multi-ethnic culture attracts professionals from around the world. Living and working together, they are highly educated and productive. The workers here are proficient in business languages, and most of them are fluent in English, Mandarin, or other languages. There are many workers from various fields of engineering. In recent years, new universities and professional schools are cultivating practical professionals with high quality. Singapore's open immigration policy contributes to its talent pool, and transnational corporations are continuously recruiting talented expatriates to Singapore from around the world.

In addition, the Singapore government spares no effort in training programs for the younger generations. It provides a large amount of scholarships for them to learn first-hand in government agencies, companies, and educational institutions, both domestic and abroad. All these efforts will ensure the distinctive competitiveness of Singapore's next generation.

- Transportation

Singapore's geographical location makes it play a leading role in international transport via land, sea, and air. This is enhanced by its investment in constructing itself as a transportation hub. Changi International Airport has more than 100 airlines, provides routes to 70 countries and over 300 cities, and has more than 6,200 weekly flights. Passenger traffic reached 53.7 million in 2013. Although it's been running for more than 30 years, Changi Airport is still evaluated as one of the world's most comfortable airports because it constantly updates itself to stay competitive. Changi Airfreight center runs 24 hours a day and provides one-stop services, ranging from cargo storage and repackaging to transportation. These innovations attracted more than 6,000 logistics management companies to Singapore to set up strongholds.

- Happiness

Singapore was rated Asia's best place to work, live, and entertain. Businesspeople in the Asia-Pacific Economic Circle depend on Singapore as an important base area. Visiting guests are courteously welcomed to make them feel like they're at home.

People from various races and religions are blending in, making Singapore a multicultural society with mutual support and a harmonious lifestyle.

Singapore's high-quality living is supported by efficient public transportation, a green living environment, high-level medical services, a sound social welfare system, and public security. It is impressive that Singapore has maintained a fiscal surplus throughout a global recession. This red dot, standing high on the shoulders of giants in the world, will become a key city of world-class investment and wealth management. In active international communication, Singapore is the shining wave on top of the tide sweeping across the global economy in the Greater China region.

CHAPTER 2

REVAMP

FOCUS ON STRENGTHS – GROWING TOGETHER ON ORCHARD ROAD

Orchard Road is Singapore's most famous tourist spot. It's a trendy shopping and entertainment center that runs through Sinagpore's central business district. Boasting several department stores, numerous retail stores, and a shopping mall with almost 5,000 brands, it's called Singapore's trendy shopping heaven.

Tourists from all over the world, coming and going around the street, present a scene that easily draws shoppers in. This shopping street, less than three kilometers long, is always changing for regular customers. It is also lined with greenery to make it pleasant for visitors who're just sightseeing.

The rise of Orchard Street can definitely be called a miracle. For the two centuries prior to stores being built here, this area was filled with orchards growing tropical fruit and farms cultivating spices and peppers on the hills. A wave of disease changed everything. By 1900, it was abandoned land filled with infested plants.

This caused Singaporeans to start a new chapter of recreation. In the 1970s, C.K. Tang, Plaza Singapura, and Mandarin Hotel opened and initiated the next page in Orchard Road history. It was transformed by renovation planning, and Orchard Road became Singapore's must-see tourist attraction.

Ngee Ann City is one of the biggest department stores in Southeast Asia. Ngee Ann City and Takashimaya department store became the anchors of this large-scale shopping center.

Orchard Road, though only 2.2 kilometers long, has three metro stations: Orchard, Somerset, and Dhoby Ghaut. This impressive shopping center is concentrated between Orchard Road and Somerset. Tourists are able to get off at Orchard station and stroll until the end of the Orchard Road.

Orchard Road is also equipped with spacious underpasses, including those that connect shopping malls, department stores, food centers, and neighbouring pedestrian overpasses. This is not only convenient but also helps to avoid tropical heat and dodge afternoon thunderstorms.

Besides discount seasons in June and December, Orchard Road has stimulated its marketing plan by developing the Singapore Tourist Authority. This allows department stores to offer great discounts throughout the year. So it is no wonder that for most tourists, a shopping spree is the number one motive for going to Singapore.

For many years, the main shopping holiday has been Christmas. It is one of the most important holidays for Orchard Road. Every Christmas, Orchard Road transforms itself into a display of lanterns. Usually the lanterns start lighting up in mid-November, and every year it follows a theme corresponding with the city's development. Different designs decorate every corner of the street.

According to statistics from Singapore Tourism Authority, in recent years Orchard Road and Marina Bay have attracted almost seven million people during the Christmas season. Those attending enjoy a highly developed entertainment system, Christmas festival events, and a New Year's countdown.

Recently, Orchard Road has seen a restructuring project of 40 million US dollars that has increased the number of streetlights and green areas. The main road has been divided by fresh flowers and plants and decorated with artistically designed streetlights. This has all occurred to create tropical scenery that would display the city's pride and create a centerpiece for the City in the Garden!

The role of the Orchard Road Business Association is to connect business activities in the district, attract people, and continue to create new business opportunities. In the future, part of Orchard Road will be changed into a pedestrian mall to keep up with the leading trends. This dream deserves our attention.

CONNECT NEW IMAGES

In the 18th century, Singapore was just another fishing village with hawkers in the streets trying to make a living. At the beginning of the 19th century, European and Asian merchants started to arrive. Slowly but surely, Singapore became a bustling trade center.

The rise of Singapore's economy is closely connected to Singapore River. This river has a long and complex history. It has built a foundation for modern trade in Singapore. Through modifications and restructuring, it has witnessed a gloriously interesting development. These days, it enables future development by embracing the leisure and dining industry.

Clark Quay is on the bank of Singapore River. It is named after Baron Andrew Clark. It offers leisure and nightlife activities. In its early days, Clark Quay mainly provided storage for Singapore's trade center. So it is no wonder that it became filled with shops, since it was a meeting point for Chinese and European merchants. The architectural style of the local buildings confirms the story of this quay. After Singapore's government restructured it, Clark Quay has transformed into a tourist attraction. Storage facilities have turned into diners, bars, shops, and clubs.

Thanks to exquisite planning, Clark Quay has kept its rich cultural background. This planning managed to combine charming historical and modern elements, which are displayed through boldly innovative methods. Fullerton Hotel, with its 80 years of history and tradition, recalls Duke Fullerton's first visit to Singapore. It brings a cultural note to this part of town. Built in 1910, Anderson Bridge is a breath taking structure on Singapore River. This bridge is a symbol of old times and the unique features of Singapore.

Clark Quay is one of the favorite spots for Westerners. There are bars and diners that catch the eye, spreading along the banks of Singapore River. One can hop on a boat and enjoy the breeze and lanterns decorating the night scenery. You can also jump on a traditional tuk tuk or just walk along the banks, enjoying the water channel and the long history enclosed in old stores and storage facilities. It is a truly romantic scene. When night falls, and the lights of the clubs turn on, you can also enjoy one of the best nightlife scenes in the world. Clark Quay slowly transforms into a bustling and lively scene that brings excitement and romance that will challenge all of your senses.

The current restructuring plan hopes to establish Singapore River as a multifunctional tourist destination. At the same time, it hopes to build distinct locations with campaigns such as "New Choices on the River". This effectively separates districts and offers the unique, respective features of Marina Bay and Orchard Road, as to attract the tourists from other scenic spots. This way, they can first experience history and then experience modernity just by crossing the river.

The vision is to connect three originally separated quays by extending it so that it would comprise of 500 proprietors, 700 companies, and 10,000 residents in total. This would unite different interests, create a platform for different needs, and consequently attract the attention of the public and media to bring new vitality to this area.

THE DEVELOPMENT OF SINGAPORE CITY IS DIVIDED INTO THREE STAGES:

(1) Concept Plan:
Population increases, as well as the future needs of the city, will be taken into consideration when restricting the land to create strategies for a ten-year, long-term plan.

(2) Master Plan:
Every five years, there will be an update, using different colors for different districts. This will designate the purpose of the area, as

well as specify the density, height, and usage of buildings. Since the last update was in 2013, the next one will be performed in 2018.

（3）Development Control Plan:

Detailed urban planning will perform or amend details. After each amending, the plan will change according to the changes in population and scope of business and life. The government is prepared to open its channels and listen to suggestions and ideas from the local public. This will result in a 50-year national development plan for the land. In the planning, a blueprint will be available with different colors marking different projects, including a commercial area, residential area, mixed area, industrial area, and 45 other areas. The public can click on the Urban Redevelopment Authority's website and easily see how many buildings can be built in particular areas and what the purposes of future buildings will be.

In addition to determination, transparent and detailed performance of the plans make the public trust governmental policies. These plans are also quite specific. In the past five to ten years, the government has been able to meet all of the demands and needs of the city. In this manner, the public can learn about future changes, identify segmenting, and predict the values generated from a long-term investment.

CHAPTER 3

EMPOWER

THE FUTURE ACCORDING TO TALENT - MARINA BAY

Marina Bay is situated at the estuary of Singapore River. It has also been created by reclaiming land from the sea. When it was developed, the whole idea was to extend the old city center, create a new central business district, and combine it with modern elements. The planners wanted to create a first-class infrastructure that offers Asian financial towers and skyscrapers, sky wheels, and marina gardens. Thus, they would build a new skyline for the city that would attract financial talent from all over the world. This piece of precious land that came from nothing would shine bright in the future and make people anxiously anticipate it.

Marina Bay is Asia's Wall Street. People of different races form a team of international financial experts here. Like New York City, it is a place that never sleeps. It offers nights full of activities to be enjoyed by people from all over the world and from every profession.

Since the beginning of the 19th century, Singapore has used its geographical advantage to slowly turn itself into an international trade port. This area has evolved throughout British colonization, Japanese occupation, and Malaysian alliances. The center of town has extended from Orchard Road to the Newton District. However, the importance of this economic source should not be disregarded. Shenton Way and Robinson Road on the southern banks of the river have become financial centers and are called Sinagpore's Golden Shoe.

In early years when travelling around Singapore, one usually took a boat from Clarke Quay because you'd been told that you would cruise along the banks of Singapore River to enjoy the mixture of old and new buildings. The boat would go to Merlion and come back. At that time, all one could see was bare land and construction yards filled with cranes and excavators working day and night. In reality, there was no scenery to enjoy. But after ten years of comprehensive management, this place has turned into the tourist and financial center of Singapore.

Nowadays, when you take a taxi from Changyi and go along the east coast and enter the city, your first impression is the spectacular Singapore Flyer. What follows are tall buildings reaching into the clouds. These skyscrapers were built on reclaimed land spreading across 360 acres. Singapore's government has used this piece of land to connect it with the central business district and turn it into a new financial center. This hidden jewel has been uncovered from the ground and allowed to shine and become a new star.

DISCOVER A WAY TO RECLAIM HIDDEN RESOURCES

For the past 20 to 30 years, Marina Bay began to stretch from Merlion to the south, inch-by-inch and through a landfill. The long-term vision, determination, and commitment to high performance regarding this project can be seen from one's whole experience with Marina Bay.

There is an old Chinese saying that it takes ten years to make a sword. Experiencing thirty years of persistence and efforts, today's Lion City can finally show Marina Bay to the rest of the financial world with pride. In the early 1970s, Singapore started its reclamation of the ground on both banks of the Singapore River estuary. After 20 years, the land for Marina Bay was created.

Since it leans on old Singapore's central business district, the Urban Redevelopment Authority has decided to closely connect Marina Bay with the city center. This expansion has created an enjoyable place where one can live, work, and play. The bay district has a first class infrastructure, including multifunctional Asian businesses, advanced financial buildings, exquisite residential buildings, luxury shopping malls, and world-renowned casinos. It also has parks, museums, and other tourist attractions that spread along the riverbank to bring that extra something to the environment.

The Urban Redevelopment Authority has set up a vision for development that abides by the principles of the three E's. Specifically, its goal is to provide people from all over the world and from different professions a platform to explore, exchange, and entertain themselves. This model of a bustling city center filled with energy has been successful and has already become reality.

- Explore:

Creative development in a residential environment. This concept provides the opportunity to enjoy unique experiences that combine work and pleasure by developing high- class residential buildings in the business area.

- Exchange:

The global financial center has already been built. This includes Marina Bay Financial Center, Asia Square, and other commercial buildings.

- Entertain:

New experiences of colorful entertainment. Marina Bay Sands Singapore attracts numerous visitors and fans. The first year it opened, it was connected with Resort World Sentosa. It has already surpassed Las Vegas by becoming the world's second largest casino in the world, after Macao. In the early afternoon, if you climb up to the rooftop gardens on one of the skyscrapers in the financial center, you are able to see people coming from all the different banks for lunch.

There is a fast and clear vision of opening a communication channel that needs effective systems and policies. This includes an operative plan for city development and the challenge to create new improvements. Only in this way will the earth's surface never lose its glamour because the stars of tomorrow will never cease to rise.

Singapore is the smallest state in all of Southeast Asia, and its population only surpasses Brunei and Timor-Leste. The greatest geographical advantage of Singapore is that it's situated on the communication point between the Strait of Malacca and the South

China Sea. However, there are other places with the same advantage in relatively close vicinity. In the early days, before Singapore was established, Malacca had already become a bustling colonial trade port.

Throughout Singapore's history, its success story has actually been achieved by leveraging its uniqueness and focusing on excellent development strategies and execution.

Singapore needs to strengthen its geographical position. In addition to lifting the level of its trade and logistics centers, it needs to establish unique competitiveness that could not be replaced by other neighboring countries. For Singapore, the financial and technology sector that creates a highly added value is a suitable direction for development. Human resources are the basis for achieving this kind of goal. In this century of Asia's rise, strategic, geographical positioning could enable Singapore to have success in the Chinese and ASEAN markets. This could attract even more multinational talent. This will allow Singapore to take its best first step into entering the global financial market.

FIND THE RIGHT FIT

Data published by Boston Consulting Group reveals that Singapore ranked third in the global millionaire density population, after Qatar and Switzerland. Impressive economic growth in recent years has made the number of millionaires in this state reach 10% of the total population. According to information published by the Ministry of Finance in November 2012, there are over 32,000 people with an annual income of 700,000 Singapore dollars (550,000 US dollars). This is only 1% of the taxed population. Among them are

Singapore's executives, accountants, financial managers, doctors, lawyers, engineers, and other professional experts.

Singapore is also the number one nation when it comes to the number of superrich people in the total population. At the moment, 10 out of every 100,000 households have assets that are higher than 100 million US dollars. Only Switzerland has higher numbers, with 11 superrich people out of every 100,000 households. Hong Kong has 7 superrich people out of every 100,000 households.

The Asian-Pacific wealth reports released by the consulting company Capgemini Financial Service and by Canadian Royal Bank have revealed that the number of millionaires has continued to grow and has reached 4.3 million people in the Asia-Pacific region. Rich people in this report were defined as persons who have at least one million US dollars to invest. That was the first time that the number of rich people in this area exceeded those in North America. It has continued to exceed those in Europe.

Reasonable taxes, transparent supervision, efficiency of government, the close vicinity of numerous other countries, a rich cultural and language tradition, and other factors have made Hong Kong and Singapore attractive places for the world's richest people. It is no wonder that these places attract ever more foreign investors and that these places are becoming more and more appealing than other places in the region.

Just as British rich people prefer the Channel Islands or American ones prefer islands in the Caribbean, Asian rich prefer Hong Kong and Singapore. Thus, these two places have become the Switzerland of Asia. They are places of gathering for foreign rich people and are consequently the center of Asia's rich people. Most of them are entrepreneurs or their successors. It can be seen that this region will continue to push the wheels of the motor of the global economy, and the trend of exceptional economic growth will make this region grow in numbers of wealthy people.

The reports also revealed that some countries in this region have become a growing market for the large-scale collection of luxury products, such as sports cars and yachts. When it comes to collections of wine and golden coins, rich people in this region have also shown great interest. China and Hong Kong have already surpassed the USA when it comes to the art and antique markets. So these results are not that surprising.

Free market, high support for business, and the density of banks make Singapore one of the most important centers for the rich. Where there is money, there is market. In this age of speculative money flowing into Asia, capital needs a safe harbor. Sinagpore's understanding of business, unusually good financial services, and safety have made this state become the first choice among the places to invest money, even on risky days.

Since it is so small geographically, Singapore does not rely on the size of its country. It relies on the power of developing its unique strengths and creating added value. It focuses on building the advantage of starting businesses and realizing dreams in this red dot. This includes integrated brands and services, which make Singapore succeed on the world stage.

When Singapore turns 50, it needs to look at how to transition in the future. This needs to start with labor and industry, turning workers into service employees with higher and added value.

This is Singapore's development model, which has evolved over recent years.

In the vision of Singapore becoming the financial center of the Asia-Pacific region, it combines content with highly added value. Besides attracting talents and investors from all over the globe, it continues to activate its own inherited talents and transforms its geographical challenges into unique strengths. Land is reclaimed from the ocean, and Singapore is changing this land into service businesses of the future.

MANAGE BY EXCEPTION

Keppel Land, Hong Kong Great Wall Business, and Hong Kong Land have invested 2 billion Singapore dollars to build Marina Bay Financial Center. This has already become a new landmark in Singapore. This center spreads across 3.55 acres and includes luxury office buildings and residential condos. These office buildings have 33 to 50 floors and offer 3 million square feet of first-class office space. These residential buildings are a centerpiece of Marina Bay.

Marina Bay Financial Center was designed by the famous American skyscraper builder KPF. The façade has an avant-garde design and was built around concept of a crystal glass curtain. Furthermore, designers have considered environmental factors by designing energy-efficient ventilation and elevators. Terrace gardens are able to effectively reduce the room temperature. In almost every part of this complex, you will be able to witness environmentally friendly ideas and solutions. Interior displays enhance the already clever design. Glass walls create the feeling of more spaciousness, provide the interior with more light, and give residents the opportunity to better enjoy the beautiful bay scenery.

An example of a residential building situated in this financial center is The Sail. This is an internationally renowned residential building built in 2008 that oversees Marina Bay. It actually is comprised of two buildings with 63 and 70 floors, respectively. The building as a whole is 245 meters high and contains over one thousand apartments. This is one of the tallest residential buildings in Singapore. The building has a glass curtain in the shape of a sail. This has not only displayed the beauty of architecture and caught the eyes of visitors from around the world, it has also initiated a series of avant-garde concepts that decorate the whole area.

Surrounding coasts complete the exceptional maritime scene. Swimming pools, gyms, tennis courts, recreational facilities, five-star hotels, and restaurants are all housed in these buildings. Residential buildings in Marina Bay provide local businesspeople with exquisite residential spaces.

Besides this, Marina Bay also offers Marina Bay Residences and Marina Bay Suites, two high class residential buildings. Due to the sea scenery and access to Shenton Way, locals call it the Golden Shoe financial district. It also boasts numerous international bank headquarters, as well as the newly built Asia Square and Westin Hotel. This all makes Golden Shoe shine even more.

Located in District 1 of the central business district, apartments in Marina, due to their crucial position, all fall under the leasehold rule of 99 years. The Singapore government has invested continuous and determined efforts to develop the MICE (Meetings, Incentives, Conventions, and Exhibitions) industry.

In recent years, Singapore has simultaneously developed an infrastructure and supporting facilities that have gained popular approval by the public. It has already become the MICE center of the Asia-Pacific region. Every year, there are an average of 6,000 commercial activities. This accounts for one quarter of these activities in all of Asia. They attract over 3 million business visitors per year.

THE MIRACLE OF GARDENS BY THE BAY

Singapore's nickname as a City of Gardens is well-deserved. In this kind of country where one needs to fight for every inch of land in continuous battle with the sea, this kind of achievement is admirable. One third of Singapore is reserved for gardens. Among these horticultural projects, the most impressive one is Gardens by the Bay, which occupies 54 acres.

When it opened in June 2012, Gardens by the Bay occupied almost 1/3 of the Marina Bay. This required investing a great deal of money and time to turn a piece of precious land taken from the sea into a garden. Singapore's prime minister admitted that this decision was not easy at all. Building a commercial or residential building in this area would have meant a fast turnaround of capital, but building a garden meant being rational and brave.

In order to realize the vision for gardens in the city, the government has embraced a long-term vision under the guidance of the city development office. Learning from Central Park in New York and Hyde Park in London, one billion Singapore dollars were invested to complete this project and make it one of Singapore's landmarks.

This garden is big as 177 football fields. As thematic forests and sceneries, the most attractive points for visitors are the Supertrees, Flower Dome and Cloud Forest.

Built from 18 steel pillars, groves are inspired by tropical rain forests. Their height is between 20 and 50 meters. These towering, unique structures are made out of various creepers and vines. Besides spectacularly designed plants, this park also collects solar energy and rain water that are distributed through a special underground system. As water feeds the plants in the park, electricity and other needs of the facility are met.

Between the groves there are bridges, which offer views of the tree tops and creeks below. And at night when the lights are on and start to mingle with the spectacular view of Marina Bay, a marvelous scene reveals itself that visitors will never forget.

Flower Dome is a greenhouse that combines a Mediterranean and tropical climate. The temperature is kept between 20 and 25 degrees, and visitors can enjoy such plants as olive trees, bottle trees, jujubes, and many other species.

On the other hand, Cloud Forest offers climates of Latin America at altitudes of 1000 to 3000 meters above sea level. Inside the dome, there is a manmade mountain, which visitors can reach with an elevator and then climb down by walking through meandering paths. In manmade mists and waterfalls, visitors will experience mountainous plants first-hand.

Lee Hsien Loong, the third and current Prime Minister of Singapore, once said that Sinagpore's urban planning has already taken the next step in its development by building its new vision of City in a Garden. Just imagine a spectacular image of a city of 6 million people surrounded by greenery, gardens, and the sea. Realizing the concept of building a Garden City is an important milestone on the pathway to this dream.

SEEK REVOLUTIONARY INSIGHTS

After he took the role of prime minister in 2004, Lee Hsien Loong encountered the government discussing the opening of casinos. The sensitive subject of gambling made the island sink into a deep conversation. One might say that this was the biggest debate over a specific public policy since Singapore was established. There was opposition not only by religious organizations and parties, but also within the cabinet itself.

But Singapore's tourism industry was stuck regarding development due to its limited leisure resources. The challenge was developing tourism activities that would be attractive to neighboring countries. After numerous discussions, it was realized that providing additional contents to the visitors in Singapore might increase their spending. Therefore, development of a resort that would include casinos became a priority.

Although this decision was much disputed and contained certain policy risks for the island, Lee Hsien Loong was determined to build the casino. Six years later, Marina Bay Integrated Resorts was built and started to operate. Besides increasing employment opportunities, it has succeeded in attracting foreign tourists. Due to transparent and efficient supervision and management, the worries about serious social, financial, and criminal issues have been carefully resolved. This is further proof that it is all about suitable risk management and the determination of pursuing success.

Marina Bay Sands was built with an investment of 8 billion Singapore dollars by America's Golden Sands Corporation. It is the world's most expensive casino. It was designed by the famous Canadian architect Moshie Safdie. Its fluent structure and bold, creative style has already made it one of Singapore's landmarks.

The infrastructure of this facility includes a five-star hotel with 2500 rooms, 12 acres of meeting rooms, a luxury shopping mall, arts facilities, a science museum, and many other buildings. Of course, there is also the world's largest casino that offers 500 gambling tables and 2500 slot machines.

Another thing that stops the breath of many visitors to Singapore is a structure that includes three tall buildings and a garden in the shape of a boat. Besides panoramic views, dinning, and other facilities, it offers the world's largest swimming pool on the roof of a tall building. It is 146 meters long and has a spectacular view since there are no walls to impede it. People are subsequently able to swim in the pool and simultaneously enjoy the bay's scenery. It is an unforgettable image.

Waterborn Trail is 3.5 kilometres long. Following the coast of Marina Bay, one can visit the tourist center, science and history museum, Youth Olympic Park, and the Singapore Flyer. Tourists can elegantly walk among sightseeing spots in the bay district and enjoy food and scenery at the same time.

Even more activities, such as National Day fireworks, New Year's countdowns, landscape art, concerts, and laser shows, turn this financial center into a giant stage during the holidays.

NAVIGATE AROUND A WEAKNESS

Every year, Singapore sees 2400 milliliters of rainfall on average. It is thus classified as an area with ample rainfall. However, since the rivers within the borders are short and shallow, there are no deep lakes that contain the water. Therefore, there is an issue of scarce water resources that have always troubled the local government. At the beginning of the last century, English colonizers built two large-scale reservoirs in the north and central parts of Singapore. At the same time, they built a pipeline from Malaysia to import unprocessed water.

Along with Singapore's development and the increase of its population, potable water became a pressing issue. In addition, after independence, Singapore's water resources stayed in Malaysia. This experience has created a sense of urgency among Singapore's citizens, so the sustainable water resources have become a number-one goal for Singapore. After a decade of efforts, Singapore has built five water processing plants, four water production plants, and one desalinization plant. In this manner, they have covered the needs of 40% of the citizens.

In 2008, Singapore built a large independent water reservoir. Its surface is 10,000 acres, and it collects the water from Singapore River, Kallang River, and Rochor River. By 2012, 17 water reservoirs total had been built. Among them, the biggest is Marina Reservoir. On the exit of Marina Bay, there is Marina Barrage. The overall dam is 350 meters long and contains nine smaller dams that are each 30 meters long.

According to estimates by the Public Utility Board, once the process of desalinization of water is complete in Marina Reservoir, it can supply ten percent of the population with potable water. This facility not only provides water, it protects from floods and serves as a leisure facility. It was crafted twenty years ago in the mind of then Prime Minister Li.

Ten years after its inception, Kallang River was cleaned. Finally, construction work started and was finished in three years. Beside the dam, there is a main building in the form of number 8. Inside the building is Singapore's Exhibition Center, in which the history and design of water resource protection is explained with multimedia and dynamic models. The roof has a grass surface the size of four football fields. Since it is distanced from the bay, it offers a great panoramic view. During holidays, it is a place for kite flying, outdoor dining, leisure, and relaxation.

Although it's not the largest dam in the world, Singaporeans' creativity, determination, and ability to overcome their geographical shortcomings is something worth admiring and learning about.

In the long run, Singapore's water problem cannot be solved without Malaysia. In recent years, Singapore has made efforts in building and planning water reservoirs and desalinization and recycling facilities in order to solve this problem before the contract with Malaysia on water supplies expires in 2061.

Singapore and Malaysia signed the first such agreement in 1927. This agreement expired in 1961. Then two subsequent agreements were made for 50 and 100 years. There have been some disagreements over the contract, and this has affected Singapore and Malalysia's relations on numerous occasions.

Singapore has simultaneously accelerated efforts in collecting rainwater, building water reservoirs, and researching the processing of polluted water. These measures have not only decreased Singapore's dependence on Malaysian water but have also provided a better position in talking with Malaysia.

Water is a top priority in Singapore. Besides having a clear goal of water management and being determined to solve the problem of lack of water, Singapore now wants to become a water supply hub in the 21st century. It wants to expand onto international markets as an exporter of solutions for water management and technology.

Singapore has been able to go from not having water to giving others water. This is thanks to their willingness to explore, gather experience, and build technology around it. People often say a crisis is an opportunity, and Singapore's experience definitely proves this philosophy of management.

MAP YOUR ROUTE TO SUCCESS

The south district of Marina Bay is divided into two parts by the East Coast Parkway Highway. This affects the development of the whole Marina Bay district. Because of this, the Land Transport Authority has planned the Marina Coastal Expressway that will go along the southern coast, extend to the eastern part of the island, and replace the current road.

The whole undersea tunnel goes along the sea dyke. It is dug 150 meters from the dyke, while the deepest part is 20 meters below the sea bed. Five lanes should suffice to support massive transport in future years. The old road will be changed into a regular town road. In this manner, the city will be able to develop toward the south and make development more integrated.

Further, the East Coast Parkway Highway will connect with Changyi Airport. In the west, it will connect to the Ayer Rajah Expressway and Jurong district. In the north, it will connect to Woodland and Johor Bahru through the Kallang-Paya Lebar Expressway.

The traffic network is built around the city center, where only five kilometers of road have an enormously strategic value. This might help us understand why Singapore's government does not skimp on these investments.

Singapore is a tiny island that has witnessed a population increase that followed its economic success. Scarce land and numerous people have created problems in housing, while industry development and commercial activities are limited. Hence, the problem of insufficient usable land has always been a problem for this country.

Land reclamation in Marina Bay is Singapore's long-term solution for scarce land. This reclamation had actually already begun during English colonization. However, at that time it was limited to the wetland of the estuary of Singapore River, and these were all small projects. The larger-scale projects started in 1960 and began on an eastern coast road that was 14 kilometers long. It continued with Jurong Island, Changyi Airport, and Marina Bay, and it is still going today.

PATTERN YOUR ACTIONS ON THOSE OF THE WISE

According to data from the Urban Redevelopment Authority, Singapore's territory will reach 733 square kilometres by 2030.

This is 151 kilometers more, compared to 582 square kilometers of territory in 1960. This has required patience, since the slow process and costly price of land reclamation may not result in the projected prosperity for 30 years.

The government is not only working to be reelected. It also has to plan for future generations, even citizens of the next century. One of its goals is to provide future citizens with an eternal home through improving laws and regulations. Short-term interests may benefit people's lives right now, but they could impact future generations detrimentally. From this point of view, Singapore's implementation and enforcing of laws is the best part of this country. Long-term visions rarely avoid short-term problems.

However, excellent leaders will make people look at these temporary setbacks in a positive way. These people are especially talented in emoting contagious enthusiasm. They are upbeat and can get others excited about what they are going to do and make them say, "Yes! We will be there!"

A clear and convincing vision will always exceed the expected results. A leader with futuristic talents is inspired by the way things could be. They energize others with their visions of the future. This makes those involved spontaneously turn into a support group that work together and devote themselves to activating this vision.

The following are the five important elements that make dreams turn reality. Create the possibilities, explore alternative ways to proceed, clearly describe the vision, concentrate on solving the problem, and understand and encourage those involved. A dream is a starting point in a city's development. It makes investors invest big because they want to experience the development.

The times we live in call for people who dare to be aware of their strengths, break the rules, and see new possibilities.

The Property Investment Department of Citi Bank Asia believes that the interest rate is now very low because rich people are still optimistic about property in Singapore. They still rely on prime locations in private residential areas and the central business district for their investments. Although foreign buyers need to pay an Additional Buyer Stamp Duty, they are still interested in exploring the possibility of owning a piece of property in a prime location.

Nowadays, the buyers will go for a more long-term investment. Instead of five years, they might prolong it to eight or ten years. The local government's hope is that they will acquire long-term investments and replace them with short-term ones when it comes to property investment.

Singapore's superb leadership is best displayed in planning and performance. This can be seen from long-term projects like the one in Marina Bay. We should learn from them with open hearts and absorb their advantages. A city's operation relies on the government to build resources. Only in this way can a city have clearly shared visions and inject new vitality into its strategic plan. Singapore opened two casinos despite a fierce debate, and a new seed was planted so that a tropical rainforest could be built.

We all strive for heroism. We think an enormous population means a great country, and big means beautiful. We have all learned this, but Singapore must not be passive because of it.

Try turning letters into numbers: A = 1, B = 2......Y = 25, Z = 26. If you do this and sum up the word ATTITUDE, you will get 100 points.

When standing on the world stage, if you are determined to use your own talent, develop your own strengths, and keep an attitude of excellence, your economic growth will always be blissful.

CHAPTER 4

NOURISH

FROM ZERO TO HERO - SENTOSA THE MIRACLE

Sentosa is an island with an area of 5 square kilometers that contains 3.2 km of long white sand beaches. Sentosa is 0.5 kilometers away from the south coast of the main island. 70% of its island area is covered by rainforest. Sentosa is a habitat for animals like monitor lizards, monkeys, peacocks, and parrots, as well as various other local flora and fauna. In recent decades, the government has increased the size of the area through land reclamation. Initially, there was only a small fishing village on the island named Pulau Belakang Mati, which means "island without offspring" in Malay. In 1967, the British returned it to the newly created Singapore government.

In 1972, the Singapore government decided to develop the island into a scenic area for domestic travel. Renamed "Sentosa", which means "quiet and peaceful" in Malay, the island got rid of its bad fortune and transformed into Singapore's most famous tourist attraction. With its new name, the island's brand image radically changed, and it officially launched the transformation with full energy. Reclaiming land step-by-step for a quarter of a century, the government implemented its original intention. It built new communities to meet the needs of the times. Eventually, amusement parks were also built there to appeal to fashionable lifestyles.

In 1974, the cable car system between Sentosa and Mount Faber was officially opened. In 1992, bridges in Sentosa were put into formal use. A sound transportation network makes it very convenient for visitors to explore the island's recreational attractions, including Fort Siloso, museums, musical fountains, natural beaches, Universal Studios, and Underwater World.

In 2006, Singapore's government made prospective, overall planning to construct the Resorts World Sentosa and Universal Studios Singapore theme park in order to revitalize tourism. All of the new construction was completed in 2011. Sentosa Express system, with a cost of $140 million, built the island anew. Tourists can easily transfer from the HarbourFront Mass Rapid Transit (MRT) Station through the Northeast MRT Line to Sentosa Express. It now only takes four minutes to reach Sentosa Island. For 40 years, Singapore's government has adhered to every stage of planning. It seemed to an outsider like Sentosa rose to fame overnight like Cinderella. Sentosa has become Singapore's most famous scenic spot, attracting more than five million tourists a year.

A LIVING, NATURAL AMUSEMENT ISLAND

As a small island in the southern tip of Singapore, Sentosa has abundant tropical rainforest resources and provides a perfect environment for vacationing. Facilities catering to different ages are taken into consideration, such as historical landmarks, hotels, nightlife, and restaurants. It's designed as a playground for all ages and contains the world-renowned Tanjong Golf Course, Fort Siloso, Merlion Park, a 2 km-long tropical beach, a butterfly park, and dozens of adventure and amusement parks.

The island has nearly 3,000 hotel rooms, as well as luxury villas. It's known as the "world's most beautiful and desirable address". You can spend an entire vacation staying on the island and never get tired of it. For Singaporeans, this is a vacation spot that you do not have to travel far for, as it's just a 15- minute drive over a bridge — easy and convenient.

Various festivals make Sentosa exotic in different seasons. Siloso Beach is 1.2 km long. A New Year's countdown party, the Sentosa sand sculpture exhibition, Halloween activities, and flower shows are held there annually. They bring constant passion and vitality to this island that encompasses only four square kilometres. Distinctive luxury hotels are open on the same block, each one unique and offering choices in a lively market. If you prefer peace and quiet, adjacent villa-style hotels in Sentosa will suffice.

In recent years, Singapore's Tourist Office has put a lot of effort into promoting international forums, prize trips, and the organization of conventions and fairs. M.I.C.E (meeting, incentive travel, conventions, and exhibitions) is one of the strategic initiatives to bring more visitors who will stay longer. This will increase the tourism business in Singapore. This has resulted in economic benefits that give reason for optimism and offer a relaxed platform for doing serious work or just having fun.

Resorts World Sentosa occupies 3.5 million square feet. It includes Universal Studios, a marine biology park, Festive Avenue, six restaurants, casinos, meeting rooms, a theatre with 1600 seats, open-air stages, shopping malls, and restaurants.

Singapore is only the second country to open Universal Studios in Asia; Japan was the first. An investment of seven billion Singapore dollars was invested in 12 major facilities. One of the facilities is the world's largest sea aquarium, which offers an explorative trip into sea life for families and children. Ocean Life Park contains 60 million cubic liters of sea water. The aquarium showcases over 800 species and a total of 100,000 marine organisms. It offers the opportunity to be face-to-face with sharks.

Festive Avenue is open 24/7. Its highlight is Dream Lake, which was designed by Jeremy Railton, the winner of four Emmy awards. This show combines flood lights, flames, lasers, and water curtains to bring its visitors a spectacular performance. Every weekend night at nine o'clock, there is a performance of "Crane Dance" on the 1300-seat square on the river bank. This performance incorporates sounds, lights, water, and dance. The open stage, accompanied by a light breeze, elegant melodies, and romantic love stories, offers the visitors of Sentosa and its coast an extra tone of excellence.

LEADING WITH THE STRENGTHS OF MAXIMIZATION AND RISKS MANAGEMENT

Singapore currently has two casinos, Marina Bay Sands and Resorts World Sentosa. Marina Bay Sands is an integrated resort fronting Marina Bay in Singapore. It was developed by Las Vegas Sands (LVS). It is the world's most expensive building at US $4.7

billion, including the cost of the prime land. Resorts World Sentosa was developed by Genting Singapore, listed on the SGX. It is a sister resort to Resorts Worlds in Genting, Pahang, Malaysia, and Manila, Philippines. The resort occupies over 121 acres of land and is one of the world's most expensive casino properties.

These two casinos can each be called outstanding, in terms of their size, investment, and business performance. In 2010, when these two facilities opened, economic numbers soared and made Singapore a global winner in the casino industry. With GDP growth close to 15%, this is the fastest since the establishment of this country.

Two corporations have created 22,000 direct business opportunities for 40,000 employees, which is around 2% of the total working population. In other words, 1 out of every 50 workers in Singapore has directly or indirectly worked at a casino-related business. These economic superstars targeted various types of guests and tourists. According to some assessments, these projects have contributed to 1.5-2% of GDP and have increased the prospects and visibility of this sector in Singapore.

These casinos offer dining, hotel accommodations, travel, and shopping, as well international conventions and fairs, dance and music performances, and other holiday activities. The taxes paid by these casinos are stunning. In 2011, they contributed over 1.1 billion Sinagpore tax dollars, which is 2.2% of the operating revenue of the local government.

On July 1, 2012, Singapore extended gambling restrictions from persons who have gone bankrupt or have received subsidies to those who have received mid-term or short-term welfare or have rent overdue for more than six months. They are all not allowed to enter casinos.

Despite this, the admission tax of these two casinos is still growing. As of 2011, each month they add up to 16 million Singapore tax dollars, which is equal to 12.6 million US dollars of admission taxes. So it is no wonder that Singapore's National Committee for Anti-gambling is constantly looking for amendments to the related laws. These amendments restrict the number of citizens who are allowed to enter a casino and thus avoid being trapped in gambling debts.

CREATING HEROES IN EVERY ROLE

Sentosa has been called the world's most beautiful residence. It is a luxury residential area on the coast. Unique, open, and safe, it is the result of 20 years of urban planning.

In 1986, Singapore's cabinet approved reconstruction of Darat Island. In 1993, Singapore's Urban Redevelopment Authority approved a development plan for a residential district in Sentosa and offered this land to developers at the price of 800 million Singapore dollars. In 2006, the first private villa was built in Sentosa.

Sentosa Island is divided into North Cove and South Cove. This polder has been organized into five small islands. Between them, there are five-foot high dams and connected water channels that are three feet high. Their total length is four kilometres. After reclaiming the island, roads and lights were installed, and trees and plants were added in two thirds of North Cove. Hence, it became an island filled with coconut groves and desert oaks.

Reclaiming land from the sea increased the surface of Sentosa Island by 25%. Most of the residences are condos or villas with terraces facing the South China Sea. It is as if the purpose was to display Sinagpore's developing strength and economic power. To live in Sentosa apartments that face the sea means to fully enjoy a sea view – from freight ships bringing goods into the port to speedboats that go to Indonesia to private yachts, tourist boats, and fishing boats. This all adds up to a bustling yet romantic scene. There is also a man-made yacht channel near Tanjong Golf Course. This creates an eco-friendly place where you can park your car behind your yacht.

Singapore is one of the global maritime freight centers, and it is one of the busiest ports in the world. Looking at it from the apartments in Sentosa, one can see loads of goods stored in the port or cruisers resting on the shores. The port sees 130 shipping companies from more than 80 countries going in and out of the port day and night. On average, every 10-12 minutes there is a boat entering or leaving the harbor, which means that each year every ship in the world's fleet docks at least once in Singapore. This is the reason that Singapore is considered to be the world's most effective port.

Close to the equator, Sentosa has a tropical climate and typically has high temperatures and sudden showers. When you add scarce water resources to this climate, it's understandable that it was just a small fishing village prior to its redevelopment. The landscape has changed since Singapore's government applied reclaiming technology, spent decades creating new land, sold this land to developers, and turned it to one of the most expensive properties in the world. It sounds like the Greek myth of King Midas turning everything he touched into gold.

Most of Sentosa residents moved there from far away. Most are businesspeople from other cultures in different parts of the world. You could call them modern nomads. But instead of wandering across water and pastures, they've moved to a tiny island near the equator for the opportunity to realize their dreams. Just like flying seeds, they've landed on this fertile land to grow roots.

Sentosa is Singapore's only coastal residential area. The main objective of the management of Sentosa is to create world-class living on a leisure island. They want it to not only be the best holiday resort, but also the best place to live. Property developers and investors call Sentosa's luxury residence area the world's most envied, desirable address.

In order to increase the privacy of the residents while ensuring they have practical and convenient living, Sentosa residential area has a reception office with guards. If you live in the building with private apartments, each resident has its own private elevator that is accessed through a personal card. As soon as you reach your floor, you are able to directly enter your own entryway or living room. That means you could own your privacy and not know anything about your neighbors even if you've been living there for several years.

Singapore's private apartments are well-equipped. They have swimming pools, Jacuzzis, gyms, BBQs, and gardens. These are considered basic amenities. They also come complete with appliances of European quality. This kind of facility makes you feel like you are on a luxury holiday.

Sentosa residential district has also developed its own hotel, shopping center, yacht club, bike path, and pedestrian trail. Hence, the planners have taken into consideration the rest, safety, and convenience of its residence.

There are more and more people visiting Sentosa every year. In order to improve the quality of transportation, the management bureau has widened the roads and increased the number of monorail and traffic lines that connect Vivo City and the main street in Sentosa. They have spent 36 million Singapore dollars to upgrade the cable car on Mount Faber, complete the second bridge to Sentosa, and effectively distribute traffic needs of the visitors and residents while in Sentosa.

Sentosa arose from nothing. It offers elite villas that are the only properties in Singapore that foreign citizens are allowed to purchase. Even though each residence in Sentosa Island Marina Residential Area is subject to a 99-year leasehold, it globally enjoys a good reputation among investors due to its smart planning and unique features.

The feeling of not caring about the world around you may be hard to comprehend, but then again, there is a saying: Not all people think the same way you do.

CHAPTER 5

GROWTH

TALES OF TRANSFORMATION – THE EAST COAST'S MAKEOVER

The Katong area was just a coastal fishing village in the 19th century. Meanwhile, there were rich Peranakan businessmen, who were the descendants of Chinese immigrants from the 15th-17th centuries, living nearby. But when Singapore's port trade emerged in the 1920s, these businessmen started moving from the bustling downtown or the riverside to the east. Then they settled down in the coastal Katong area and built up Southeast Asian-style villas.

These villas partially inherited European architectural features. They blended Mediterranean window shades with Malaysian doors and Chinese lotuses and bat totems. This created a fusion of architectural styles. Commercial shops opened along residential areas and formed a busy settlement of businesses and residences. Nowadays, when walking along East Coast Road and Joo Chiat

Road, you can still see all the well-preserved Southeast Asian-style buildings.

In Singapore, the government's detailed urban development plan strictly protects all of these buildings, as well as luxuriant old trees. When starting new construction, builders are responsible for maintaining monuments and considering them throughout the architectural process. With numerous trees scattered among the new buildings, a quiet elegance tells stories about the history of the area.

Stretching across 15 kilometers with a total area of 185 hectares and surrounded by the scenic coastline, East Coast Park is one of Singapore's most popular attractions. Developed about 30 years ago, this park attracts more than 7.5 million visits per year. Its restoration project from 2007 to 2010 was carried out with a total budget of 160 million Singapore dollars. Visitation is expected to reach more than 8 million people during 2015.

East Coast Park's developing theme is Recreation for All. The park is divided into different areas, including a large open space, four fitness equipment activity areas, 80 barbecue pits, and a rental center for bikes and skates. The park features a bike trail that goes along 12 km of the coast, a 15 km jogging track, a 7.5 km sandy beach, a water sports center, tennis courts, volleyball courts, a parasailing pool, a foot massage center, walking paths, and an extreme skateboarding park. There are additional options for sports fans, where you can enjoy the fun of outdoor activities on the East Coast while you practice your skills.

The annual International Marathon is held regularly here. Runners or bikers can exercise along the coast all the way to

Marina Bay. On Park Avenue, the trees, sea breeze, and outstanding facilities combine together to make an excellent space for runners. At night, after a busy day, you can sit by the beach and watch the fishing lights from a distance. Or you can go to the East Coast Seafood Center and enjoy delicious food and beer.

The beautiful overpass and underpass easily connect nearby residential areas with East Coast Park. The cozy East Coast is only a 15-minute drive from the busy Marina Bay Financial Center, which makes it convenient to get a change of scenery and pace.

In 1970, the Singaporean government started reclaiming land from the sea to build the East Coast Parkway (ECP). This changed the appearance of the whole area tremendously. The ECP starts at Changi Airport and extends 20 kilometers to the east. In the first 15 minutes that passengers travel into the city, people can see grand, nicely trimmed trees that stand along the sides of the highway and welcome guests. The median island is made of neatly trimmed bushes, including colorful bougainvillaea or plants of the season. This gives guests the first impression of the City in a Garden.

When heading into the city, you can see modern, private mansions with more than 20 floors standing on the right side of the ECP. On the left side, the East Coast Park stretches along the east coastline. Since the airport, coast, shopping centers, and workplaces in Marina Bay are within a 15-minute drive or bus ride, the park becomes a beloved place for both locals and foreigners.

East Coast settlements are quite different from other areas. Mostly rich foreigners or local business persons occupy Sentosa, Bukit Timah has towering trees, and Marina Bay is the financial center. Now on the East Coast, there are also emerging villas and convenient Housing and Development Board (HDB) flats. Chinese, Indians, and Westerners are the main ethnic groups moving into the East Coast. Most Chinese residents have been living here for generations. The new immigrants can easily get along with the locals as long as they are willing to, and no one cares which language you speak.

In *The Future and Its Enemies*, Virginia Postrel writes: "Do we crave predictability, or relish surprise? These two poles, stasis and dynamism, increasingly define our political, intellectual, and cultural landscape."

Singapore's urban planning is famous throughout the world, and it can be divided into two parts: its conceptual blueprint and master planning. The conceptual blueprint directs the development of land and transportation, so that people can imagine what this city will look like 10 to 30 years from now. And based on the blueprint, people can see the master planning that clearly marks and accurately calculates the public facilities, transportation networks, and industrial layout in both densely and sparsely populated areas.

Population growth must be taken into consideration with urban planning, and Singapore's government has paid special attention to the balance between dense and sparse populations in every area. In Singapore, infrastructure is always a priority in city construction. This focus mostly comes from financial allocation and bidding investors. For example, in the development of an industrial park, the infrastructure will be constructed by developers, and the relevant government agencies will take it over after completion.

Furthermore, during the process of property development in all countries, the cost of tearing down buildings is increasing, which affects the costs of real estate. There are a lot of policies and measures to learn from when tearing down property in Singapore. There are two vital concerns:

1. The new property that people move into must be better than the property they were staying in.

2. After tearing down a property, keep some memory of the building that was there intact.

This way when people see that their living environment is improving, and they simultaneously have a reminder of their past. Then they will support the government's action in removing the building, even though they feel sentimental. This helps sustain the healthy development of Singapore's real estate market.

Tradition and change on the east coast of Singapore continue to shift and affect each other. City development plans always give citizens confidence in the balance between stability and motion.

In order to share fortune and fiscal surplus, Prime Minister Lee Hsien Loong announced the "Remaking Our Homeland" plan in 2007. This plan included rebuilding more infrastructures in the city in order to improve our homeland. The National Development Department spent 1 billion Singapore dollars over 5 years to implement this city development plan. The plan is mainly about building infrastructures in residential areas, beautifying the environment, constructing new houses, and bringing life to the city.

Singapore is an island country with a large population and small land area. It has almost no resources and limited possibilities of expanding the land. However, the needs of people are constantly increasing. The biggest challenge of the Singaporean government is to find balance between stabilized life and active economic growth. It needs to leverage limited resources while people's incomes increase.

Through years of hard work, the Singaporean government tried to solve the ongoing problem of its citizens, so that the real estate market could develop in a way that would keep up with the rapid development of the economy. The City Reconstruction Bureau set up two councils separate from all other functional departments. They were named the General Planning Council and the Development Control Council. They helped develop the plan for the city in a reasonable and orderly mThe General Planning Council includes representatives from major public construction departments. Its function is to coordinate land requirements for each public construction plan, so that it will be carried out as soon as possible. Members of the Development Control Council include representatives from professional organizations and public services, mainly the Environmental Division. This council is in charge of major development programs of non-public sectors. This includes simultaneous long-term and short-term planning, so that stability and activity continue to develop in harmony in Singapore.

THINK GREEN

The color scheme of a city is very powerful. It provides a clear positioning of the city, as well as an advantage that other cities cannot catch up with in a short period of time. You can separate the experience of a city into simple individual elements, which causes competition with each other to improve. Singapore's plan to be the City in a Garden uses greening to surround all architecture of the city, which showcases its uniqueness.

The coverage rate of greening in Singapore is 70%. 9% of the land is planned to be kept as natural reserve areas. There are 44 parks that cover 20 hectares. The total central parks of the city, which cover 3 acres, have 1.1 million trees, over 11 million bushes, and 4,868 hectares of green space. Even buildings and overpasses are planned for greening.

From the 1970s through the 1990s, Prime Minister Lee Kuan Yew insisted that Sinapore plant 20,000 - 30,000 trees every year in order to practice the policy of greening. During that time, Singapore was poorer than other countries in Asia. The topic of environmental protection seemed irrelevant. He still insisted that Singaporeans follow through. Almost every corner that a tree could be planted in has trees growing. After 40 years of hard work, today the public green areas exceed 9,500 ha, which is about 13.6% of the total land of Singapore. Of this, more than 3,000 ha are classified as Nature Reserves. This has caused Singapore to be listed as one of only two cities in the world that has a primeval forest. Trees that are two or three stories high have become the most beautiful decor of buildings, as well as air purifiers of the city.

The National Park Board now manages more than 40 parks, takes care of 1.3 million trees, and many more million shrubs. About 3,000 types of trees have been planted in the urban landscape, and over 70% of them are introduced species. That likely means that Singapore has the most biodiverse landscape of any city in the world. Every tree in Singapore is numbered, and each one is attended to regularly, which includes trimming and eradicating pests. The main goal of greening programs is to keep Singapore green.

Nowadays, a new dimension to the green space has been introduced to the city. There is an increasing adoption of skyrise greenery, which includes rooftop and vertical plants in newly iconic buildings like the National Library Building. The Integrated Resort in Marina Bay encourages Singapore to step into a new greenery era. One can not only play in the parks and reserves there. In the very near future, one will be able to live and work in the greenery garden.

If you live in or are visiting Singapore, you should try just slowing down and enjoying the gorgeous trees growing toward the sky. The trees in Singapore are immaculately taken of, and residents and visitors should really enjoy their presence. When Singapore successfully became a citywide garden, someone suggested that it be called the "City in a Garden".

In order to keep this vision going in Singapore or realize it in your own community, you can contribute to a green environment by investing in green energy projects to reduce power consumption. In Singapore, the National Park Bureau expanded the covered area, provided a cash allowance, and released the Skyrise Greenery Incentive Scheme. This encouraged existing building owners to set up vertical greenery or a green wall by planting trees, flowers, roof gardens, or other greenery.

The roads in Singapore take up 12% of its land area. No matter where you are, you will find a public bus station within 300 meters. The numerous bus lines transfer to metro lines, and they are all well connected with shopping street and food centers.

The most common means of transportation in Singapore is the public metro system, also often referred to as the SMRT or subway. The first metro line started building in May, 1982. It has 42 stations and cost around 5 billion Singapore dollars to build. The 67-kilometer subway line connects south and north Singapore. It runs along the busy Orchard Road, connecting Yio Chu Kang Road and Toa Payoh. It was put into use on November 7th, 1987, which was two years ahead of schedule.

In September, 1995, several organizations and departments merged and established the Land Transport Authority, which manages the metro, road construction, and public affairs of transportation.

OWN A DREAM HOUSE

There are three types of real estate in Singapore. Namely, they are private property, Executive Condominiums, and houses planned and constructed by the government department called the Housing and Development Board (HDB). Private property can be divided into landed residences and non-landed residences. HDB houses and Executive Condominiums both have a 99-year leasehold. Private property has three different types of titles or deeds, which are 99-year, 999-year, and freehold. Some types of residences include detached, semi-detached, terrace, and shophouse.

Singapore's government was concerned about foreign investors buying private land, starting to speculate it, and subsequently taking control of the development of the country. To prevent this, the government specified that only Singaporean nationals are allowed to purchase landed residences. And if you own a private residence in Singapore, you must apply to the Singapore Land Authority and provide related data. This includes the owner's professional qualifications, work experience, or investments to prove that you have made long-term contributions to the country's economy. You can only receive a Land Dealings (Approval) Unit after you're approved. Then you can purchase a landed residence.

Non-landed residences are divided into condominiums and apartments. Condominiums often have more open space and amenities than apartments, such as a swimming pool, gym, BBQ pit, tennis court, garden view, and 24-hour guards.

THE FIVE TYPES OF LAND USAGE

Tenure can be divided into Freehold and Leasehold. The former will own the property through all generations, while the latter has ownership during a limited period of time. This period depends on the different duration of the title or deed.

The price of a property will also vary. Freehold and 999-year leasehold condos are more expensive and can maintain better value. They are usually the favorite of Singaporean locals, which is because freeholds are becoming less and less of an option. For instance, near metro stations and in the Marina Bay and Sentosa areas, the only leaseholds that are offered have a 99-year duration. Also, if the government needs to build a road or rebuild something, they will change freehold land into leasehold land and offer it to developers.

Singapore has very limited land resources. Because of this, strict land control is implemented. 88% of the land is owned by the government, giving it the power of cost control over the land. They divide the land of the country into nearly a thousand sections. Each section has detailed land planning. The usage of land is divided into five types by function:

1. Industrial land, which is usually provided in the form of bid invitations

2. Activity space, which mainly refers to open spaces that are used for relaxing and recreation by the residents of the area

3. Resident area, which separates neighborhoods into smaller planning divisions, then sets up a complete supporting plan to control types and density of construction in the area

4. Transportation land, which gives priority to the urban underground rail system

5. Central business land, which prioritizes the development of finance and encourages the construction of tall buildings to improve the usage of land

Due to limited resources of land and the demands of population growth, the price of real estate will definitely increase over the long term. In Singapore, government building developers are in charge of the housing supply. This department belongs to the National Development Bureau. One of its functions is to design different HDB residences for different income levels in order to satisfy residence needs for all citizens. Citizens can purchase HDB house through a fund, which means low-income citizens can also receive a subsidy from the government.

Therefore, Singapore is one of the countries that has one of the highest rates of individual residence ownership. Over 80% of Singaporean citizens and permanent residents live in properties run by HDB. Either they live in apartments planned by HDB, or those who are more financially stable will switch to purchasing landed properties or private condos in order to achieve their goals of investing or collecting rent as their passive income.

In recent years, the vast majority of the prime locations in the city center and surrounding metro areas have all become state-owned land. The land for construction that have been released all have a 99-year title or deed since they are convenient locations with easy access to public transportation. People's everyday needs can be satisfied, so these plans are welcome in the market. There are other contractors that sell houses in the form of a 99-year leasehold, although the land is freehold. They also get quite a lot of buyers. Obviously, buyers' mentalities have changed.

Normally for houses that have been on the market for 20-30 years, developers will collect the sale of most of the residence buildings and compensate the price gap. For instance, leasehold holders that have 60 years of usage rights left can top up land usage prices for 39 years. Then they will get a brand new 99-year leasehold. Generally, freehold properties have better real-estate appreciation potential in the market.

GET THE RIGHT THINGS DONE

Singapore has a complete legal framework, and its laws are strictly implemented. People generally obey laws and take them seriously. Singapore has the same business practices as older countries, and it treasures implementing agreements.

Singapore's government has strict legal control over residential management policies, including the greening of buildings, the definition of usage areas, the duties of management councils, the sales and payment methods of pre-sale or finished property, and the house-delivering process. Moreover, it forbids false advertising, as well as business people misguiding customers. It even forbids using sample houses to mislead potential buyers or pressure customers during purchasing.

Furthermore, agents cannot represent sellers and buyers at the same time. In Singapore, if an agent is found to collect brokerage fees from both a buyer and seller, it is considered a violation of the law. Offending agents will be charged 25,000 Singapore dollars or serve one year in prison. This strict penalty is enforced to avoid the manipulation of pricing, which would damage the interest of the involved parties.

Since the transaction rate history is public and current, people can easily check this information online. Therefore, there is no big floating space when negotiating prices. Additionally, the purchasing agreement and transaction procedure are strictly controlled by the government. Customers can make rational purchasing decisions in a safe and transparent environment.

Private buildings usually provide a free parking spot for each residence. At delivery of the private residence, a closet, AC, kitchen appliances, and bathing facilities are usually included. The house owner can move in or rent the residence by simply installing lights and curtains. This eliminates a lot of inconvenience, such as furnishing the house from scratch.

Further, the law guarantees a free one-year warranty after delivery. The developers will send over maintenance staff to make repairs at private buildings for one year. Any problems occurring or defects found during this time will be addressed quickly.

KNOW YOUR MARKET

Real estate agents in Singapore conduct their business without any storefronts. This is different from retail stores of joint operation in other countries. They are under the strict control and management of the Council of Estate Agencies. However, since the laws and regulations are sound, people abide by them. There is not much to worry about regarding others manipulating a real-estate transaction, except for the standard investment risk that one is responsible for.

Factors that affect the price of real estate include the population structure of the area, external political stability, economic environment and prosperity, location of property, structural design, market price trends, landscaping, convenience, and amenities.

Singapore is a rich country. With the immigration policy expanding in recent years, it attracts a large number of mid and high-level management talents. Millions of immigrations have an urgent need for residences, and floating capital has brought a global rush into Asia. Subsequently, an environment has been created with low interest rates and low taxes, and the need for real estate has been brought back to life.

The Chinese play a vital part in Singapore's real estate business. A lot of Chinese businesspeople choose to purchase property in Singapore because "it is a safe place to park their money". According to HSR International Realtors, a local real estate company, Chinese buyers always buy more than one private residence – one for themselves to stay in and one to rent. The latter is an investment, and the owners rent it out while they're waiting for it to appreciate. According to the famous American financial news media channel

CNBC, Chinese businesspeople love to invest in Singapore. This is because they trust Singapore's public security and legal system.

In the past eight years, the number of Singapore population has increased by over 1 million. As of June 2014, Singapore's total population was 5.47 million, including 3.87 million residents and 1.6 million non-residents. In addition, Singapore is determined to become an international investment management center. This has attracted even more immigrants, which has further stimulated the need for private residences.

CHAPTER 6

TALENTS

TURN THE KEYS TO SUCCESS — SKILLS, KNOWLEDGE, AND ATTITUDE

Bukit Timah means "dense forest on the hills" in Malay. Bukit Timah Road is the longest street in Singapore, stretching 25 kilometers from south to north. Along this road is Bukit Timah Nature Reserve. It is located in the center of Singapore and occupies 1.6 square kilometers.

The reserve contains over 840 species of plants and trees, which exceeds the number of species in North America. These plants and trees connect to the ocean and provide the city with ample rainfall and rain water, as well as help the air in Singapore stay clean. The reserve has also solved the problem of extreme heat so typical of tropical areas near the equator.

Bukit Timah district isn't as developed as other residential areas. Until the MRT system has been completed, it's not as convenient or accessible. However, it is close to numerous famous schools, embassies, and Singapore Botanic Garden, which is a protected natural area with 2,000 species of orchids. Because of this, it has become the most preferred living area for diplomats and local high- level managers.

The many elementary and middle schools in Bukit Timah have become famous as places for nurturing the future leaders of Singapore. Their parents are aware that excellent results require a suitable environment.

DEVELOP TALENTS FOR THE FUTURE

Singapore is known for its good legal system, honest bureaucracy, complete infrastructure, and English language environment. Because of this, over 7,000 world companies call it home. In recent years, Singapore has achieved great success, particularly in terms of improving its economy, education, and quality of living.

Good leaders wanting to fulfill their visions must be aware of their strengths and implement the following strategies for success:

1. Nurture a group of innovative dreamers as future leaders.

2. Concentrate resources and investments on construction with visible advantages.

3. Realize that dreams will only come true if you dare to take risks and recognize disadvantages.

4. Explore the strengths, maintain the balance among "What am I suitable to do?", "What am I good at?", "What do I want?" and "What am I supposed to do?".

5. Do not let short-term obstacles weaken long-term development or the value of your vision.

6. To increase added value of your plan's development, establish unique, long-term value and avoid short-term competition.

7. Use employees with different cultural and historical backgrounds, and provide incentives to contribute through free development.

8. Throw a long line to catch a big fish. Great city development requires lifelong commitment from its citizens.

9. Establish a platform where the dream of each person will be respected.

10. Create a favorable influence that will bring you loyal supporters through enjoying the vision together.

Generation XYZ (also known as the Genius Generation) has already been established. Now is the time for creating a new generation for the future. In this new era of the world where there are no borders, workers are closely connected to each other. Because of this, experts are having difficulty predicting what the next generation will look like.

Younger generations live where there is work. It is increasingly difficult to predict how these next generations will define words such as "dream", "investment", "work", or "home". Interaction between countries will increase. All we need to do is open our hearts, be creative, accept the ever-changing world, and adapt to an international atmosphere. Then we will be able to nurture leaders of the future.

How can small countries compete with larger ones? The most effective method is to establish a system that ensures the most efficient methods for the best results. If you want to do your best in each project, excellent human resources are crucial. Under this assumption, each young man or woman is an asset to his or her country. With the assistance of hardware and software, foreign students will join with them. Together, they will become the force to push the wheel of progress even further and make this red dot even stronger in the world. This is another way Singapore leverages its resources and turns them into strengths for success.

INVEST IN YOUR OWN FUTURE

Each year, the Swiss Institute of Management Development publishes the World Competitiveness Yearbook that ranks and analyzes the ability of nations to create an environment in which enterprises can compete. In 2014, Singapore emerged as the third most competitive economy in the world and the most competitive in Asia. A small country with scarce resources and a low population has been able to excel amongst fierce global competition. It is truly a remarkable achievement.

In the past fifty years, Singapore's success has grown exponentially. This is due to a systemic display of effectiveness, force, and adequate application of its own strengths. It started with manufacturing and expanded to trade. Now Singapore is one of the world's leading regional centers for manufacturing.

This was possible not only because of the government's vision and effective enforcement. It was also due to excellent human resources that are a crucial element in Singapore's future. So an excellent education system is the cradle of this crucial element of Singapore's success.

The World Economic Forum's 2009-2010 global report on competitiveness has ranked Singapore's education quality as number one in the world. For a child about to start school, this is the place that's mostly closely connected to the entire planet. Children can learn Chinese and English at the same time and grow up in an environment that's bilingual or even multilingual.

Singapore's school system has set English as its primary language. Depending on the district, Chinese, Malay, or Tamil is the secondary language. This system makes students feel free from national boundaries while learning. It also makes them ready for the development of the world's future.

High school students in Bukit Timah make the top 10% of national rankings when taking the Primary School Leaving Examination. The government also funded the International Language Center, which provides a high level of professional foreign-language learning. This includes French, German, Japanese, Indonesian, and Arabic. Through teaching skilled multilingualism to Singapore's future elite, these students will have no problem with international standards. They will be ready to perform on the global stage, whether that be international trade, education, diplomacy, or politics.

The predominant language in Singapore is English. This is supplemented by a bilingual education policy. Students with knowledge of their mother tongue and a strong cultural identity can gain an ability to speak English language and expand their horizons at an early age. These superior communication skills, in addition to an international perspective, makes it easy for Singaporeans to study abroad. Graduates are also able to enjoy the performance advantages that come with seamless integration into European and American cultures.

Because of all these advantages, in recent years, Singapore has attracted many foreign students from the rest of Asia. Some of these students study in Singapore as a springboard to western countries, while others choose to stay in Singapore to complete their higher education.

Singapore's strategy for attracting outstanding foreign students is giving them favorable secondary school scholarships and proper life care. This is not so much an industry of attracting overseas students to earn a foreign education. It is more about recruiting talents to Singapore as a win-win strategy.

NURTURE FUTURE LEADERSHIP

In 1978, under the direction of former Prime Minister Lee Kuan Yew, a comprehensive research review of Singapore's education system was undertaken. This report was distributed the following year. One reason for poor student learning results was that the current teaching methods could not provide a curriculum that would fit the needs of students with different learning abilities and interests. So the government conducted a systematic academic reform, which introduced the concept of triage education. Although the local school system utilized the changes, it still generally remained within its original model so as not to shock everyone involved.

At the age of seven, Singapore's children start attending school and receive six years of primary education. Because outstanding academic performance causes increased enrollment, the choice of school became a main concern for parents.

Singapore has an affiliate system similar to the British, which involves teaching educational concepts. New students in primary schools can inherit their father's, mother's, or sibling's alumni advantage and enroll directly into the schools they attended. In the future, when they take an exam, an affiliate relationship can be a plus for students entering a relevant national high school. This system can create a bond among students that lasts well into their working careers. Unity coalition forces are entrenched. Through this kind of mutual trust, unique workplace cultures can evolve.

By focusing on talent development, Singapore attaches great importance to education. In the pursuit of elite education, the Ministry of Education is second only in expenditure to the Department of Defense. Education accounts for about one-fifth of total government spending. Due to historical background, Singapore inherited its education system from the British. But Singapore has also maintained focus on upholding the spirit of the Chinese. These two influences form a blend of Eastern and Western cultures that is integrated into the education system.

Singapore's corporate and public offices often require school reports starting in primary school. Since the course of education involves the entire process, they don't want to just see the highest degree. They believe that basic education is the beginning of one's personality and learning development.

Frankly, this is a very complex and delicate design for an education system. It emphasizes diverse and flexible teaching, focuses on differences in student aptitude and abilities, inspires students' potential through an individualized approach, and utilizes expertise and resources to achieve the utmost purpose of education.

Singapore's level of quality in basic education is listed among the best in the world. School principals and teachers are of the highest status. Public school teachers are considered civil servants. They receive training and management directly from the Ministry of Education in every facet and aspect of education. There are several options in Singapore, including English schools, Chinese schools, independent schools, and international schools.

In addition to learning languages, the way to educate the next generation is to place an emphasis on extracurricular activities. This provides students with the opportunity to understand the development of strengths. During the four years of junior high school and two years of high school, they must actively participate in one or two extracurricular activities, such as outdoor sports, water sports, orchestra, armed guard, or scouts. These activities will be included as a significant portion of the assessment of the academic system. The results of these studies will contribute to their advanced school performance.

One purpose of extracurricular activities is to actively cultivate teamwork. Led by a professional teacher, students use their spare time on holidays and weekends to participate in community exercises. During vacations, most kids don't participate in coursework, but they do continue to participate in extracurricular activities. This encourages children to cultivate interests while they're playing, which is a principle of education relevant to both academic and extracurricular activities.

Singapore is the regional education hub in Asia, and as such it attracts many students from China and Malaysia. Foreign exchange is a huge endeavor for the country. Singapore also recruits elite students, providing scholarships and tuition assistance to those that are willing to stay and work locally. This is creating a new generation of talented Singaporeans that will work hard for their whole lives.

Another reason to praise Singapore is its internationally recognized, high-quality health care system. According to statistics, there are over 40 million visitors to Singapore each year, and many of them are present because they trust the quality of health care.

Singapore has seven public hospitals, as well as private hospitals and other clinics. In the entire country, there are around 16,000 doctors. This means there is not only an impressive level of medical care, there has been no effort spared in the development of medical education and research.

The only problem to consider right now is how expensive the cost of medical treatment can be. In order to prepare for contingencies, health insurance companies have begun to focus on guaranteeing quality of life and enforcing risk controls. These progressing and improving public service policies will further enhance Singapore's medical system and take its quality of life to the next level.

CHAPTER 7

HOTSPOT

THE RISE OF MALAYSIA – EFFECTIVE ACTIONS

Singapore is the most googled country in the world, and neighboring Malaysia is listed as the sixth most googled country.

Centuries ago, Europeans and Indians came to Malaysia for gold, tin, and timber. Admiral Zheng-He made his first fleet of six visits to Malacca in 1405. After that, Chinese merchants began arriving at the port and pioneered foreign trading bases in Malacca. With the support of the Ming Dynasty, the Malacca sultanate consistently expanded into the rest of Malaya. This opened the way for the establishment of friendly relations between Malacca and China.

Due to the conversion of the Sultan, Islam became prosperous in Malacca at that time. Before long, Islam pervaded throughout Malaya, Sumatra, and Java. The Portuguese, Netherlander, and British occupied Malaysia in succession after the 15th century.

Malaysia came to its independence in 1957, but a racial conflict between the Malaysian and Chinese broke out in 1969, especially in Kuala Lumpur. Later, the government actively eliminated the tension between the Malaysian and Chinese. A peaceful and cooperative atmosphere among the multiple races remains today.

There are several races in Malaysia, including Malayan, Chinese, Indian, and aboriginal. Generally speaking, Malayan people maintain hold over the government, but Chinese people manage the economy. Village settlements are the center of Malaysian society. However, the government values collective responsibility. This conservatism is rooted in devotion to Islam.

Islam is the state religion of Malaysia, though the constitution guarantees freedom of religion. Most of the Chinese are Buddhist and Taoist, and Malaysia also has many Hindus and Christians. However, every Malaysian is regarded as Muslim when they are born until they decide they want to be part of a different religion. Islam carries great weight in Malaysia.

From 1981 to 1997, Malaysia's economy grew over 8% a year under the leadership of then Prime Minister Datuk Seri Mahathir Bin Mohamad. Then the Asian financial crisis occurred. Today, Singapore is one of the smallest yet most successful countries in the world, but Malaysia can be regarded as one of the countries in Asia with the great potential.

Malaysia's territory area is 329,845 square km. It consist of 13 states and 3 federal territories. The population was 30 millions in 2012, which is 86 people per square km.

Malaysia has great diversity in its landscape. There are lofty mountains, beautiful islands, and tropical jungles. Verdant palms are all over the country. Most people live a leisurely life. The coastal areas are mostly flatlands, while the central area are plateaus of tropical rainforest.

West Malaya spans 740 km from north to south and 322 km from east to west. The coasts are cut off by the Titiwangsa Mountains. East Malaya is across from Borneo. Its coastline reaches a length of 2,607 km, and its landscape includes beaches, hills, river valleys, and inland mountainous areas.

Crocker Range starts in Sarawak and runs across the center of Sabah. It then heads north, dividing into two parts. At 4,095.2 m, the highest peak is Mount Kinabalu, located in Mount Kinabalu National Park. It is also the World Heritage Site of the United Nations Educational, Scientific, and Cultural Organization (UNESCO).

The largest caverns in Malaysia are the Gunung Mulu Caverns in Sarawak. There are also many islands. Labuan, off the coast of East Malaysia, is the largest. Malaysia has a tropical rainforest climate, hot and humid. Monsoon season is from April to October in the southwest, and the northeast monsoon is from October to February. The average annual rainfall is 250 cm.

As one of the founders of the Association of Southeast Asian Nations (ASEAN), it is rich in resources, and its political situation is stable. Malaysia has a promising future.

Malaysia's living environment is similar to Singapore's, and Singapore's urbanization is similar to Hong Kong's. However, Hong Kong is firmly tied to mainland China, so Malaysia's real estate has become very attractive in recent years. Along with Singapore and Hong Kong, Malaysia was once a British colony. Its political structure has followed Britain's, as it was deeply influenced by them. Investors find that real estate in Malaysia is relatively underestimated. Thus, it has a strong possibility of appreciation.

LEVERAGE YOUR STRENGTHS

In recent years, Malaysia's neighbors like Singapore, China, and Hong Kong have imposed restricted policies on real estate investments. This makes Malaysia more popular to investors since it has a positive policy. Compared to the international market, the housing prices in Malaysia are more moderate. The rental yield in downtown area is rational, which attracts foreign investors to Malaysian real estate. Thus, the focus of investments has become second homes in Malaysia. The three most popular investment hotspots are Kuala Lumpur, Penang, and Iskandar.

Things will never go wrong for investors when they put their money into the center location of a nation's politics and economy. Malaysia is very good at planning and articulating what they have to offer.

In 1991, then Prime Minister Mahathir presented his "Vision 2020". His goal was for Malaysia to become an autarkical, prosperous, industrialized country by 2020. More recently, current Prime Minister Najib Razak distributed his Economic Transformation Program for 2010 through 2020. The program plans to invest 444 billion dollars. Furthermore, Kuala Lumpur and Klang Valley are the center of the program.

There are three national goals of the program:

1. Bring in 100 top-level international enterprises.

2. Construct the Klang Valley Rapid Transit, which will reach the length of 141 km.

3. Build a high-speed railway from Kuala Lumpur to Singapore. The speed of this train will reach up to 280 km/h.

After the reconstruction project, Kuala Lumpur is projected to be the world's 20th most economically developing city and the world's 20th most liveable city. The superior conditions in Kuala Lumpur will support it to become an international metropolis.

KUALA LUMPUR – CITY OF PROGRESS

In Kuala Lumpur, trees shade the street, skyscrapers are everywhere, and jungles surround the grand Islamic buildings. Cultural diversification is presented incisively and vividly in Malaysia's capital. The three primary races - Chinese, Indian, and Malaysian - work in cooperation, yet they remain their own unique cultures.

Kuala Lumpur is the gateway to the Malay Peninsula. There is a short dam between Bandar Johor Bahru and Singapore, which is only 1,038 m wide. The transportation between the two countries is very convenient, which means there is liquidity of people on both sides.

Malaysia possesses tropical customs in a multi-ethnic society. It attracts many foreigners that work, live, and settle here. A tropical country has a lots of advantages. What are other reasons why people would want to leave their home countries and settle in Malaysia?

Malaysia has stable politics, a harmony among multiple ethnicities, freedom of religion, and kindness among residents. These are the main reasons that foreigners are drawn here. There is also a high quality of living, including world-class education, medicine, and shopping malls. It also offers international catering and year-round sports activities, such as golf, tennis, soccer, and diving. People can enjoy a luxurious life at a low cost in Malaysia.

There are world-known buildings and tourist attractions, including the F1 speedway, the Twin Towers, idyllic islands, historical sites, and primitive beaches. These draw people's attention who are traveling around this region.

The GDP of Singapore is among the best in the world. With a lower operating cost, Malaysia can gain the most marginal benefits. As the center of Malaysia's culture and economy, Kuala Lumpur will step forward among fair competition. To fully change Kuala Lumpur and propel it to become a modern international metropolis before 2020, the first thing to do is increase the population. Kuala Lumpur's goal for population growth is to reach 10 million people by 2020. It also hopes to provide 4.2 million more jobs by then.

The government of Kuala Lumpur plans to restructure the economy to attract more international enterprises. The first priority is to build more landmarks in Kuala Lumpur. Then the traffic network will be constructed, including a high speed railway between Singapore and Kuala Lumpur. It will connect Singapore, Kuala Lumpur, and Penang from the south to the north. The planning and construction of Mass Rapid Transit will be realized in phases during the urban planning of Kuala Lumpur.

PENANG – ISLAND OF POTENTIAL

Penang is a newly rising area, located in the northwest part of the Malay Peninsula. It's divided into Penang and Province Wellesley by the Selatan Strait. The <u>Penang Bridge</u> connects the two sides. Built in 1985 with a length of 13.5 km, the bridge ranks the 4th longest in Asia and the 9th longest in the world. The <u>Penang Bridge</u> links directly to the PLUS highway on the west coast, which leads north to Bukit Kayu Hitam and south to Bandar Johor Bahru. Moreover, Penang can connect directly to Kuala Lumpur to the south by taking the railway from Butterworth Province Wellesley. One can also go north to Hat Yai and Bangkok, Thailand, on the train.

Georgetown, the capital of Penang, is the third largest city in Malaysia. Among the several developing cities in Malaysia, Penang is the farthest from Singapore, but it's the city whose culture caters to it most similarly, especially Penang's foods and deserts. The rapid, steady growth of Penang has attracted foreign investors, who are flocking there. The stable political situation and abundant employment opportunities there exhibit quite a promising prospect.

In 2013, Yahoo published a list of Eight Great Places to Retire Abroad. Penang ranked 4th and was the only city in Asia on the list. The British surveyed Penang and gave it an award for The Best Urban Council.

Here is some information about Penang's outstanding achievements in economy and industrialization:

- The economic growth of Penang ranks first in Malaysia.

- 36% of the investments in Malaysia are in Penang.

- 35% of the export of Malaysia come out of Penang.

- 66.67% of medical tourists come to Penang.

- More than 700 international enterprises carry out their business in Penang.

- Penang has been selected as the primary city to invest in.

- Penang has the best financial condition in Malaysia.

Penang Island is the focus of Penang, which is the center of political and economic activities. Although it's only a tiny island, just half the size of Singapore, Penang has an extremely high percentage of Chinese, who can speak both Mandarin and Hokkien.

UNESCO designated Georgetown as a World Heritage Site in 2008. It's an ancient city, which has abundant historic cultural features and a promising future to develop. Penang's government has been praised for being the most honest and upright local government in Malaysia. It also spares no effort as far as environmental protection. Apart from being the most livable city and the most attractive tourist destination, Penang is the most popular city in the government program called Malaysia's Second Home. Because of Penang Island's lack of landmass, the government's project to reclaim land from the sea will create more jobs.

Penang Island and Province Wellesley belong to a state on the northwest side of the Malay Peninsula. Penang Island is 285 square meters, which is only half the size as Singapore. A lot of people live in this small but prosperous area. The population of Chinese amounts for half of the population of Penang Island.

With thriving business activities, the total population is also increasing. It is estimated that Penang Island will have 2 million people by 2020. There is a strong demand for real estate due to the population increase. This will add capital flow from local and overseas investors, and Penang Island has had great real-estate performance in the past five years. The investment rule of Penang Island is a "sea view is the best". Coastal areas like Batu Ferringhi and Tanjung Bungah on the north of Penang Island are tourist areas with luxury restaurants. There are also quality residential areas where people focus on their quality of life. Therefore, foreign professional managers and local, high-earning residents are attracted to live there.

ISKANDAR PENINSULA - NO NATIONAL BOUNDARIES

In the past, Malaysia regarded Singapore as its main competition. It worried about resources exchanged with Singapore. It was also concerned that Singapore's projects to reclaim land from the sea and expand its national land could bring harm to Malaysia.

The ongoing progress in Malaysia cannot be hindered by national boundaries, domain divisions, or cultural divides. The regulations of competition among countries have been altered by the new era in which we live.

Due to the trend of globalization, Malaysia and Singapore have decided to join hands and substitute competition with cooperation. The countries have integrated global investment resources and established the Iskandar Special Economic Zone. This will allow the entire peninsula to support each other in fulfilling their ongoing dreams of growth and prosperity.

The Iskandar Special Economic Zone is located on the southernmost tip of Malaysia; about three times the size of Singapore. It is a significant milestone in the prosperity of Malaysia's economy, which frequently interacts with Singapore's economy.

Iskandar is only separated from Singapore by the Straits of Johor. This makes Iskandar the gateway to both the Europe-Asia trade waterway and the economic trade between China and India.

The Iskandar Special Economic Zone is in the developing triangle of Singapore, Malaysia, and Indonesia. It controls the pass from the Indochina Peninsula to Malacca. The zone includes an international airport, two large harbors, and a highway network. Thus, every main economic region in the world can rapidly access it by land, sea, and air routes.

Also in the Iskandar Special Economic Zone is the city of Johor Bahru. Living expenses in Johor Bahru are lower; its rent is less than one third of Singapore's. Many people work in Singapore and live in Malaysia. The Johor–Singapore Causeway is a great advantage for people that live in Johor and work abroad. Cultures on both sides are quite familiar with each other.

Thus, the potential of the Iskandar Special Economic Zone is very hopeful. The zone integrates the main cities in South Johor, including Johor Bahru, Pontian, Senai, Pasir Gudang, and NusaJaya. This region has been divided into five flagship areas. Each area bears a particular economic mission that complements the others. One can travel throughout the main cities in Malaysia through its nationwide transportation network.

The Iskandar Special Economic Zone is the largest sole developing project in Malaysia's history. According to the initial vision of the Comprehensive Development Plan, Iskandar will transform into a thriving metropolis with a lively culture integrated with entertainment and commerce, and it will develop continuously.

Being separated from Singapore by just a strip of water, the Malaysian government also wants to simulate the development mode of the Shenzhen special economic zone. This will be separated into five phases, which is estimated to take 20 years. They plan to invest 380 billion Ringgit to build Iskandar so that it will be similar to Shenzhen.

The younger generations of Singaporeans generally receive a higher education. They are not fond of manual labor like manufacturing. On the contrary, the finance, management, and hi-tech service industries are more popular. However, the salary of Malaysians is not even half as high as that of Singaporeans'. When taking into consideration that Iskandar is only 15 minutes by car from Singapore, manual labor in Singapore is becoming more and more accepted by Malaysians.

According to the data from World Bank, nearly 300,000 Singaporeans immigrated out of the country in 2010. 100,000 of those chose Malaysia as their new residence.

Businesspeople and residents of Johor are all happy about Singaporeans coming to shop or invest. According to data from the Malaysian Tourist Administration, around 24 million tourists come to Malaysia every year. 10 million of them come through the Johor Bahru portal that is connected to Singapore. If every one of the five million Singaporeans goes to Malaysia twice a year, it will be a huge business opportunity for Johor Bahru.

The ever-growing tourist trade from Singapore will drive the Iskandar Special Economic Zone to become a new tourist stronghold. A floating population of thousands means increased business opportunities. The index of consumption will imperceptibly drive the modernization of the city. "Work in Singapore and sleep in Johor Bahru" will become a more common phrase.

This means that people will earn Singapore dollars but spend Ringgit. Singaporeans will take advantage of the fact that the commodity price in Malaysia is only half as high as that of Singapore. Through the way we communicate and interact, people in Malaysia will also be able to enjoy the opportunity of economic development.

The ever-growing job opportunities in Singapore will also help Malaysia to develop into a country of higher income. It is estimated that due to new economic growth, the market will need a labor force of 5 million. With the future needs of hi-tech talents, Singapore and Malaysia can complement each other's labor forces and get what they need.

JOHOR BAHRU – A STRATEGIC LOCATION

Johor Bahru is a town of strategic importance in Malaysia. The town has the Malay Peninsula behind it and the Johor Channel in front of it. It is a transportation hub whose nickname, "the south portal of Malaysia", was given a long time ago.

In the middle of the 19th century, it was a small fishing village in Malaysia. In 1866, Sultan Abu Bakar named it Johor Bahru. Under his management, the town gradually took shape as a business town. Back then, a lot of Chinese from Canton, Fujian and Hainan also came there. Through the effort of over a century, Johor Bahru ultimately became the second largest city in Malaysia.

Johor Bahru is located at the primary location for people from Singapore to enter and exit Malaysia. It attracts a significant amount of foreign visitors every year. Those entering Malaysia from there account for nearly half of the visitors to the country. Low commodity prices and convenient transportation have also made Johor Bahru Singaporeans' favorite foreign destination for shopping and vacation.

Currently, Johor Bahru has a population of 1.6 million and is the administrative center of Johor. Its major economic activities include financial service, retail business, and sightseeing. Electronics and food processing industries also thrive there.

Around 70,000 people commute between Johor Bahru and Singapore through the aforementioned passage. Public transportation includes buses and trains. The Malaysian national railway (KTMB) train station moved to Woodland, Singapore, in 2011. In order to increase efficiency and compensate with the increasing traffic flow, the Rapid Transit System that will be built in Johor Bahru plans to connect with the Thomson Line MRT in Singapore. This will be finished in 2018. Then Johor Bahru will be the transfer station, and whole Iskandar region will be brought into a convenient MRT system between Singapore and Johor. This will benefit the development of the whole area.

A BEAUTIFUL NEW WORLD

The spotlight of the 21st century has moved slowly from Europe and America to Asia. In the 20th century, Southeast Asia went through a long, difficult period because of historical and social challenges. Nowadays, the region has political stability and economic advantages, and the countries have started to shine.

Given time, Southeast Asia will surely become a vital part of the economy of Asia.

In order to know Asia, one must know the rising ASEAN Free Trade Area. It includes the six founding ASEAN countries (Indonesia, Malaysia, the Philippines, Singapore, Thailand, and Brunei) and four new member countries (Vietnam, Laos, Burma, and Cambodia). This is a total of 10 countries with a land area of 4.5 million square kilometers, and a population of 600 million people.

In recent years, ASEAN has developed a new plan, which is ASEAN 10 + 6. This means that ASEAN wants six more countries to join - China, Japan, South Korea, Australia, New Zealand, and India. If one wants to enter Southeast Asia, Malaysia is located at the center of everything and is a good entry point with a reasonable price.

Through a construction plan of the infrastructure over the next half-century, Malaysia is moving toward becoming a modernized country. Thanks to its geological location, abundant resources, and stable political situation, it surely will be one of the future stars of Southeast Asia.

The plan to transform it into a special economic zone has made the whole country eager to realize the vision of prosperity by 2020. Even though Malaysia has a conservative immigration policy, the Malaysia My Second Home (MM2H) plan offers foreigners and long-term residents a ten-year visa and other benefits. This will create new investment opportunities for international business.

The MM2H plan will create an international focus on Malaysia. It offers a channel for people who want to retire, arrange for their kids to go to America or Australia to study, or invest in real estate in Malaysia. The weather is comfortable, and resources are abundant. If a resident's rights expire after ten years, one can apply for an extension. This offers foreigners the chance to find investment opportunities in Southeast Asia and build a second home.

Regarding economic development, the five-year economic development plan is now in its 10th phase. Transportation and public services are now at the scale of a modernized country. Furthermore, Malaysia has abundant resources and few major natural disasters. This all contributes to realizing the government's vision by 2020. This vision will help build Malaysia into an industrial country with a GDP of US $300 billion, and it will have a top ranking in fields like economy, education development, and social welfare.

Although Malaysia features an immense area and a sparse population, the government never encourages new immigrants. Compared to some countries, it is not easy to get a permanent residence in Malaysia. However, in order to satisfy the needs of foreign capital, the government has carried out policies to attract foreign investments. MM2H is no doubt an eye-catching one.

Once approved, an investor can have a ten-year long social visit pass. This measure does not affect the immigration policy but can introduce foreign capital. So far, this has caused over 20,000 people from all over the world to apply for participation in this plan.

Due to the informal immigration policy, MM2H attracts different kinds of people. The majority of people who apply meet the following criteria:

- Retired people:

Malaysia is famous for its temperatures that make it feel like summer year-round. Even when it rains, it just feels like autumn. There are no earthquakes, typhoons, or other natural disasters in the country. It is a Commonwealth nation, so people can live and communicate using English. There are a lot of Chinese people, so one can also communicate in Chinese. Additionally, it has beautiful scenery, a low commodity cost, and complete medical infrastructure. Therefore, it attracts senior citizens from Europe, America, Singapore, China, Japan, South Korea, and other Asian countries.

- Parents seeking an international education system:

Malaysia has a 20-year history of implementing dual degrees for college. Some universities have cooperative programs that offer the option of transferring credits to universities in Europe, America, and Australia. The students only need to get a domestic education or go abroad for their junior year to get the exact same diploma, which is issued by the headquarters of schools. Since the expense will be much lower, it suits parents that want to send their kids abroad but need an affordable budget.

- Property investors:

Property investors handling MM2H will have a higher mortgage credit limit. It will be easier for them to handle business properties or conduct investment research. However, investors must note that since the Malaysian government tries to protect the residence rights for its local people, they will have a different minimum investment amount and separate tax policies. And these policies are subject to change at any time.

Titles of Malaysian properties can be divided into freehold and leasehold, depending on the location. Specific titles usually involve a 99-year leasehold, which can be returned to the government at the expiration of the usage life.

Malaysia is a low-density population area. Without considering the external factors of the market, the property value of a 99-year title will depreciate over time. Unless it is in an irreplaceable prime location, investors should first consider purchasing properties with "freehold rights". Furthermore, landholding can be separated into land title and strata title. And there is another type of property rule which has been put in place to protect native Malaysians. Foreigners are not allowed to purchase the land in Malaysia, only the building.

Malaysia is on the rise. As a founding member of ASEAN, Malaysia saw the development mode of Singapore and used it as its benchmark. After it was politically stabilized, Malaysia took advantage of its abundant resources and large area and worked hard to become a developed country. With all the major construction happening around the country, the future of Malaysia looks very bright.

SUCCESS

FOCUS ON STRENGTHS

As the world progresses, social and business trends are dramatically moving toward Asia. Economic growth causing Southeast Asia to become global business leaders within the next few decades is unusually clear. The choices made by the governments of Southeast Asia have caused these trends to occur. The powers-that-be will decide if these trends will manifest if they continue to make smart choices. As an individual, you can also choose to explore your strengths, discover a clear vision, embrace changes, empower abilities, catch on to trends, and become one of the movers as the world evolves.

Step forward and dance with the vision of Singapore and Malaysia. Over the past half century, the economy in many countries lit the flame of hope for reviving Chinese society. Following the reform and opening of mainland China, economic development swept across the world. The rise of China is no longer just a hope for the future. Rather, it is a dream come true. The people of Asia have a right to stand on the verge of a trend and be happy and proud.

By focusing on the spectacular economic performance of countries in North Asia, one can see that the large habitation of Chinese in Southeast Asia is also contributing to future development through collaborating with other diverse nations overseas. In southeast countries, such as Singapore and Malaysia, the large population of Chinese has helped these countries leverage their limited resources and become prosperous nations. This is a proud historical milestone for people of Chinese descent.

Through decades of continuing effort, Singapore made the best of its limited opportunities. It turned its natural drawbacks into merits. By flexibly applying leverage to an intelligent economy, the small country was soon able to step onto the world stage.

Singapore never hides the fact that it is a small red dot of a country, nor does it ever compromise itself out of consideration for larger nations because it is small. It shines and thrives among powerful economic entities such as China, the U.S., the U.K., Japan, South Korea, and Middle Eastern countries.

Singapore holds an outstanding political vision, and it maintains action and persistence toward achieving this vision. People do not harbor a feeling of injustice because they live in a small country. Rather, they dream big and try hard to maximize their strengths so they can achieve their vision.

Singapore's leaders show people how to face dilemmas like resource shortages. They plan according to the expectation for life, collaborate with each other, and live up to the meaning of life. Meanwhile, the citizens support and cooperate with the plans of the government. Everyone works hard together to build a homeland and live up to life's purpose, and this occurs in different stages of development.

Lee Kuan Yew used to tell a story about planting trees. He would say that when a tree is deeply rooted in the ground and starts spreading out its branches, it will look ugly and messy for a while. One must have patience and wait for the tree to become lush. Then after you trim it, it will be a big tree eventually. This is the patience and wisdom of practicing vision.

Singapore and Malaysia have forged a new relationship as neighbors due to change. Maylasia is a Muslim country, and their religious beliefs are a priority. The Malaysian people do not want to give up their relaxed lifestyle. However, they have slowly opened their doors to the unknown outside world under the pressure of world development, especially China expanding their "territory".

In changing times, boats either sail faster, or they could find themselves facing a dangerous wave. Successful navigation requires the wisdom of a captain who can observe and make the right decisions. The flow of time will surely bring a vision of the future.

Do you see the power of vision in transforming Singapore and Malaysia? The persistence of the leaders of Singapore and Malaysia have demonstrated to the world how they can create a better future for their people. In order to realize the dreams of a small red dot, you have to win people's trust.

People are great because of their dreams; a great city cannot live without a great dream. This is articulates the experience of building and chasing dreams by activating its strengths. As dreamers, we also hope to help people reposition and review their own life experience. Without vision, Singapore would have never achieved everything it has, and Malaysia wouldn't have gained a new era of vitality. However, without the awareness of inherited talents and correct execution, a beautiful dream will only become a horrible nightmare. Only dreamers who take the right actions achieve their visions.

The processes of experiencing empowerment will initiate a structure for the creation of positive energy to guide decisions about your business and your life. By knowing your strengths, you will be able to motivate and lead yourself effectively.

No matter what your goals are, there will be times when things don't work out the way you want them to, and you'll feel unsatisfied. The sense of demotivation can discourage the intention of trying a new way or committing to any new change.

However, goals can also make us feel empowered and content. There are three basic human needs: relatedness, competence, and autonomy. Relatedness strengthens your relationships, competence develops new skills, and autonomy reflects upon your passions. These are intrinsic motivations, which will light the fire and fuel the positive energy it takes to be successful.

In the *Unlock the Power: 90-Day Challenge* workbook, you'll find powerful coaching questions to guide the development of your 90 Days Challenge Workbook. Sharing your vision and reflecting on these questions will help you clarify your needs and values. After you have developed your action plan and blueprint for your future, you will begin a new chapter of your life.

Get started by changing your life today. Explore your value, be aware of your strengths, and create a vision. Then get your larger vision started by accomplishing smaller goals. The process of chasing dreams creates a wonderful journey for the future.